Winter House

Winter House

Charlotte Moss

WRITTEN WITH Jennifer Cegielski

PHOTOGRAPHS BY Jason Dewey

ART DIRECTION AND DESIGN BY
Dina Dell'Arciprete | dk Design Partners Inc, NYC

CLARKSON POTTER/PUBLISHERS
NEW YORK

Published in the United States by Clarkson Potter/Publishers, an imprint of the Crown Publishing Group, a division of Random House, Inc., New York
www.crownpublishing.com
www.clarksonpotter.com

Library of Congress
Cataloging-in-Publication Data
Moss, Charlotte.
Winter house / Charlotte Moss.—1st ed.
1. Interior decoration—Psychological aspects.
2. Winter. I. Title.
NK2113.M67 2005
747-dc22 2004026175

ISBN 1-4000-5438-9

Printed in China

Design by Dina Dell'Arciprete

10 9 8 7 6 5 4 3 2 1

First Edition

Acknowledgments

Thank you, thank you . . .

Building a house requires electricians, plumbers, cabinetmakers, painters, and other craftsmen, and a book comes together in a similar way. Without a wall, there would be nothing to paint, and without photographs there would be less to write about. Without snow there would be no *Winter House*.

I would like to thank Jason Dewey and his photographic assistant, Brian Porter, for the countless hours we have spent together in my house photographing the rooms and their details, countless table settings, and Christmas decorations over several winter seasons. We have run around Aspen taking pictures and walking with the dogs along the Roaring Fork. Most important, I am grateful for their flexibility and for their being on call to capture the house under a fresh veil of snow. I would also like to thank Pieter Estersohn and John Hall for the photographs they contributed along the way.

Art direction and styling could not be executed without Dina Dell'Arciprete, as she always sees unique photographic possibilities in the tiniest detail and combinations of things. Her graphic eye always leaves me humbled. I also have Dina to thank for introducing me to Jennifer Cegielski, who no matter how tight the deadline smiled and got it done. She took my tapes and crafted the text, at the same time providing me with her own ideas, which were always balanced and thoughtful.

Behind all the creative madness it is absolutely essential to have someone who is calm and well organized—that would be Jessica Everhart. In addition to cataloging and recataloging every photograph, organizing and reorganizing all the photographs by room, and keeping me (and everyone else) on deadline, Jessica pulled everything and everyone together to make all of our lives easier.

Michelle Canning used her decorating skills to organize, complete, and catalog all the decorative schemes, help to create new schemes, track down resources, and work with Dina, Jessica, Jason, and Jennifer on all aspects of this book.

Everyone at Charlotte Moss Interior Design contributed in one way or another. Hannah Noble and Claudia Barston assisted in wrapping gifts for photo shoots, researching, and hunting down resources. Heather Randell was minding the store, keeping track of contracts and finances. Caitlin Rutkay also helped in researching room schemes. Shane Hobgood tried to keep me on track and on deadline, and Ricky Spears and Jennifer Marsico cheerleaded and did whatever was needed to keep the process moving. Somer Bingham assisted Jessica in sorting the photographs, and Marie Dauphin smiled calmly when the rest of us were crazed. My thanks to Catherine Carlson and May Gardner Keegan for their patience when I had to be on a photo shoot and not in the office decorating.

In Aspen, thanks go to David and Denise Clark for always managing to find the flowers and plant material that I wanted and for consistently coming up with arrangements that amazed me; to my wonderful and very patient housekeeper, Arcelia Torres, for helping me set and reset tables, fixing lunches, keeping the coffeepot full, and returning the house to perfect order, always with a patient smile; and to Ken Clayton, our caretaker, who pitched in to do anything and everything, from moving furniture to running errands.

Once a book is written and photographs are taken, the baton is passed to another team. I would like to thank Lauren Shakely for the opportunity to write this book, and the rest of the team at Clarkson Potter: Natalie Kaire, editor; Pam Krauss, editorial director; Marysarah Quinn, creative director; Sibylle Kazeroid, senior production editor; Linnea Knollmueller, production manager; and Maria Gagliano for editorial assistance.

As always, I thank Phyllis "Ducky" Wender for always believing, and for always rendering sage advice.

And last, but never least, thanks to my husband, Barry, for his patience when the house has been completely turned upside down, with people always present, buckets of flowers in the hallways, and rooms marked "off limits"—he always managed a smile, just as he has done for the last twenty-three years.

Thank you all.

Contents

9 Introduction

CHAPTER 1

17 Make Yourself at Home

Welcoming Gestures

Gathering Rooms

Public Areas

CHAPTER 2

59 A Space of One's Own

Private Quarters

Guest Retreats

CHAPTER 3

119 Decorating for Fun

The Holidays

Trimming the Tree

The Table

CHAPTER 4

161 Enjoying Yourself

Staying Inside

Heading Outdoors

184 Resources

187 Scheme Suggestions

188 Room Scheme Details

189 Recommended Reading

190 Index

SKI & SNOW COUNTRY
Ski Style
MCBRIDE & BLACK
Lartigue's Winter Pictures
Flammarion
le ski et ses modes
PORT
CHARLOTTE MOSS
Charlotte Ann Moss
SISTER
P

“You can’t just live a little bit—you gotta give it your all.”

MARY WELLS LAWRENCE

Introduction

MORE THAN JUST A HOME, A WINTER HOUSE IS A FRAME OF MIND. It is here you can retreat, relax, recharge, and reconnect with friends, family, and—last but not least!—yourself. In a way, a winter house has a split personality. It is full of life and laughter when loved ones gather to share in the good times of the holidays or come together to recap and recuperate after a day of activity outdoors. But it is also quiet and calming, where a half day dedicated to reading a book is a reality and time spent in a fragrant herbal-infused bath is more an après-ski necessity than a luxury.

The physical location might be a second home where you go on weekends or vacation, but you don't necessarily need *another* house to have a winter house. Nor do you need to make a major financial investment—simple seasonal decorating changes can transform your home and get you in the winter-house spirit. A switch to cozier slipcovers on the sofa and vases filled with wintry flowers and greenery will help transport you to another place. You can apply many of the concepts in these pages to almost any home. But wherever and however you choose to create your winter house, the important thing is that once you come in from the cold and close that door behind you, you have found a retreat.

My own quest for a winter house began, paradoxically, in the summer. My husband, Barry, happened to be golfing in Aspen when he called me in New York and said, "It's even more gorgeous here in the summer than in the winter." Knowing that he wanted a ski house, I replied, "Maybe we should get a house there?" He was speechless. Having grown up in the South, I didn't have firsthand experience of what a winter house might be like (when I was a child, we always went to my grandmother's place at the river or to Virginia Beach as a getaway), but being a decorator I welcomed the opportunity and the challenge. We had been going to Vail for years for different corporate events and had visited Aspen a number of times to ski. We were amazed at what the small town nestled at the base of a mountain had to offer. We loved the real heart and soul of the place, and there was plenty to do beyond the slopes. So it was decided: we would look for our winter retreat in Aspen, and off to Colorado I went. The original plan was to keep things simple. My mission was to find a cozy condo—we didn't want another full-size house and all the maintenance that goes along with it. Little did we know there was a house waiting there just for us.

I spent a whole day touring different condos with our Realtor but didn't see anything I liked. We were just about to head back to my hotel when our Realtor asked if I'd like to stop and see a house that was for sale. With the voyeuristic thrill that comes along with the territory of being a decorator, I said, "Why not?" Now, having been in and around all manner of houses with clients throughout my twenty years in the design business, there is one truth I know to be self-evident—when you are looking for a house, and you find the right one, you know it. You *feel* it. When we pulled up in front of the house he wanted to show me, I said, "Looks great." We stepped inside and I said, "Looks great." We kept looking around and I said, "Looks great." A eureka moment. I thought, *If this house looks this good in the summer, I can't wait to see it blanketed in a shimmering coat of Rocky Mountain snow.* In my mind I was already enjoying a pot of my favorite tea by the magnificent stone fireplace. As you might have guessed, that very same house is the house you see in this book.

I was immediately drawn to the evocative, romantic mood of the house. It is in a residential neighborhood and close to the street, but iron gates set between stone walls give it an air of privacy. An anomaly amid the original Victorian style of the rest of the town of Aspen, this house could very well have been a chalet hanging on the side of a mountain somewhere in the Alps. The moment you step onto the path, you're surrounded by wonderful textures to please the eye—the wrought-iron balcony and gate, the bluestone walkway, the stacked stone walls, the patina on the copper cladding of the windows and doors, the thick blue-gray shingles made of rustic distressed wood, and the deep blue-green antiqued shutters. It was a place where I felt immediately at home, and to this day I still look forward to every visit in every season.

Once we closed on the house, things started to happen pretty fast. It was August and we wanted to have our winter house ready for its first ski season in a few months. The idea was to create a comfortable escape for the two of us, our family, and our friends, and we planned to make the most of the house's wintry charm every year from Thanksgiving through the last possible weekend of spring skiing. Luckily, the house didn't really need much work other than some tinkering with bathrooms and, of course, making it our own. I threw myself into decorating it and was excited to be able to use design ideas that had been floating around in my head for some time. With the weather and the season when we would be occupying the house in mind, I sought a saturated, textural decorating style, with lots of patterns and even layers of patterns on patterns. As we counted

down the months to opening weekend, I never passed up an opportunity to take a look around antiques stores I encountered in my travels, and my basket of favorite fabric swatches was an essential resource for inspiration. And, as my own decorating client, I was able to make decisions very quickly. Once you start a dialogue with a house and you see how the rooms lay out, everything just sort of flows. In this case, the result was an alpine/French provincial combination, with lots of French country antiques, Irish pine, and painted furniture. Several underlying winter-house motifs developed—woodland flora and fauna on hand-painted china, Black Forest elements and horn accents, artwork capturing people skiing, skating, dancing (in other words, having a good time!), and other winter-related imagery. You don't know when or where you're going to seize upon these themes, but somehow they end up finding you—I call this decorating serendipity.

Because guests are an integral part of any winter house, we made sure we had plenty of guest rooms. As these pages illustrate, each took on a distinct personality. And while we love being in the house alone, my husband and I also look forward to the times when the guest rooms are chock-full of family and friends. These visits are a time for everyone—holiday company, weekenders, skiers, painters, even those who simply yearn to relax or read—to do what they want and come together to have fun. A winter house is too good not to share.

Make Yours

elf at Home

“The house stamps its own character on all ways of living; I am ruled by a continuity I cannot see.”

Elizabeth Bowen on Bowenscourt

1

Make Yourself at Home

WELCOMING GESTURES GATHERING ROOMS PUBLIC AREAS

As someone raised in the South—a region rich with a long tradition of hospitality—I learned early on that the most memorable homes are the ones in which you feel welcome. From the moment you step over the threshold, and often even before you do, these homes seem to embrace their inhabitants, visitors, and living itself. You instantly feel a sense of ease in everything from the overall arrangement of a room to the smallest gestures of comfort. And while any house should be warm and welcoming, this feeling is essential in a winter house that you often share with guests.

Though you may greet people with the words "make yourself at home," you can extend this invitation in many unspoken ways as well. Guests first experience a sense of welcome outside as they come up the front walk and then when they enter the foyer. Inside, the main gathering rooms take over and winter's cold gives you all the more opportunities to add welcoming touches. In the living room, extra throws blanket the sofa and comfortable chairs are clustered to invite relaxed conversation and provide a cozy place to gather. Dinner tables are set to say "this meal is special" and encourage guests to pull up a chair. Even the kitchen is a place to feel comfortable, where you are totally at ease to make yourself a pot of tea to carry up to your room. Public areas like hallways and powder rooms can welcome guests in their own way, too, with objects and artwork to entertain the eye. And everywhere, the "little luxuries" of fresh flowers, beautiful books, candlelight, fragrance, music, and treasured personal possessions set a relaxed mood. Many of my favorite little luxuries are suggested in these chapters.

Welcoming Gestures

As guests approach our house from town, they are first greeted by the natural beauty all around. Aspen Mountain rises overhead, and the Roaring Fork River cuts through the land. Ours is a quiet neighborhood, and people generally pull up right in front of the house. It is from here that the welcoming begins!

The soft glow of a lantern (above) and candlelight (opposite) anticipate the arrival of guests in the evening. The doorway is dressed with fresh-cut evergreen garlands to echo the surrounding landscape. The antique iron gates are topped with an embossed iron crest adding a dash of ceremony at the entry.

THE EXTERIOR

I always consider the first impressions new visitors will have when they see the outside of the house. When I am expecting someone, I like to throw open the iron gates as if to say "Come on in!" A second opportunity to welcome guests is when they come down the walkway and up to the porch. I think the impact of this approach is at its best and most beautiful for a winter house after a fresh snowfall. The snow muffles everyday noise and softens everything it touches as it blankets the gates, and stone walls, along the front of the house. It's a mysterious, magical effect, almost like being transported back in time. When everything is monochromatic outside, the warmth, light, and color inside draw people in and make everyone who walks through the front door feel more welcome than ever.

If you were to visit this house in the warmer months, you'd see a small grove of aspen trees and shade plantings on one side of the front yard and a winding path leading to a traditional English perennial border on the other side. Of course, at this time of year they are just a memory. It's true that most of the garden is at rest during winter, but there is no excuse for not having something green dressing up your home and gardens to make things look alive and festive. Garlands draped around the door and sometimes around the columns of the front porch echo the surrounding landscape and give everyone coming and going a breath of fragrant evergreen. For me, that's always the smell of the holidays. These garlands go up in December and stay through the March spring-skiing season, with a bit of "sprucing up," so to speak,

One winter, red berries punctuated the greens of garlands and window boxes.

along the way. Window boxes filled with evergreen boughs contrast nicely with the shutters and the shingles; if you don't have window boxes, you might fill large planters on your porch, stairs, or lawn instead. I prefer to change the winter decorations each year, experimenting with different palettes and materials. One winter, red berries punctuated the greens of garlands and window boxes. Another year, when I wanted a peaceful scheme of green and white tones, I filled zinc tubs on the porch with birch cuttings tied with evergreen bunches. Lanterns and wooden snowflakes danced above for a three-dimensional display. The simplest additions, such as bare branches painted white for contrast, can create an entirely new mood. For a smooth transition from the outdoors, whatever you have going on outside can set the theme for that year's indoor decorations and Christmas tree.

When I entertain or decorate for the holidays, I set candles and lanterns along the path. From a practical point of view, they light the way up the walk; from an aesthetic point of view, I love the reflection of the flickering light in the snow. Larger lanterns on the porch sometimes hold subtly scented candles to treat guests to a gentle waft of additional fragrance. Dressed like this, a house establishes a festive mood and one of anticipation—even a little bit of ceremony—before people arrive at the door.

Garden containers can be filled with different wintry themes to suit your mood. A fantasy forest of birch branches (opposite) graced the front porch planters one season, while window boxes overflowing with greenery changed their look over the months with the addition of festive berries (right) and other colorful branches.

Why stop at decorating a tree indoors? Barren outdoor branches get in the spirit with a few ornaments of their own. I loved the feeling of "snowflakes among the snowflakes," and the crystal beads captured the light beautifully.

THE FOYER

When I walk through the door, I feel a sense of release. I'm thrilled to put away my work files and reconnect with the house, and I can't wait to crack open a new book, plan a dinner party, or whatever else it is I've got on my agenda. It's a feeling of "Hallelujah, I'm here!" and, of course, I want all who enter to feel the same way.

From the outside porch, guests are ushered into the foyer. I'm right there at the door to say hello—this house is that kind of place and Aspen is that kind of town. I believe that every entrance hall, large or small, should create a big sense of welcome. Once they're inside our foyer my guests are also greeted by something to see. The Portuguese console table is usually topped with a delft vase, a Black Forest cachepot, or a Swedish majolica vase filled with whatever is in season. The arrangements are more naturalistic than fancy—large white amaryllis tucked among evergreen and eucalyptus clippings, for instance. This white-and-green color combination is a good option when you want a wintry look. Every evening a scented candle burns to warm the air in contrast with the outdoors. A hall table is also a temporary stopping place for the endless array of mail and packages that seem to flow in and out of a winter house during the holidays. I tuck all the Christmas cards people send around the edges of the framed French mirror above the console or place them in a basket to decorate the foyer. What guests wouldn't feel welcome when they discover a card they've mailed thoughtfully displayed?

I always prefer fresh flowers in the foyer; as an alternative to one container try using several similar containers of different scale, grouping a few together with complementary flowers (opposite). To control cold blasts of air from entering the living room, paisley portieres edged with a wool loop trim tucked into the seam (above right) frame and soften the doorway.

Although the rest of the area is furnished like a room, with watercolors of English landscapes and a needlepoint stool, it is designed to be practical for winter activities and a busy household. Our foyer is really an expanded hallway that connects the front and back of the house; the same stones lead up to the porch and head down the foyer into the living room, so your eye follows along and draws you in. Because the stone floor is low maintenance, you can just kick off your ski boots without worrying about scratching the surface, and inevitably boots line the hallway. Extra storage for all the cold-weather gear is necessary in the foyer of a winter house. A closet can hold things people might need to borrow—coats, mittens, the odd pair of skis—but a hall tree with a "winter wardrobe" of scarves and hats is both practical and visually appealing in an entrance hall. My antique iron Victorian model, a gift from a client, becomes a kind of seasonal sculpture: in the summer straw hats and baseball caps replace wool and fur ski hats. The dog leashes can always be found there, too.

Elements from a winter wardrobe—warm hats, Nordic sweaters (right)—become part of the seasonally revolving décor in the foyer, while English watercolors of country views (opposite) are a more permanent installation with a gallery effect.

…your eye follows along and draws you in

Gathering Rooms

One of the most remarkable aspects of a winter house is its ability to draw people together, and I find that there are three main common areas where everyone naturally tends to congregate: the living room, the dining room, and the kitchen. These bustling centers of activity are the heart of your winter house (or any house, for that matter—what is it about the kitchen?).

I wanted the main seating area to have all the essentials: a comfortable sofa, chairs placed for conversation, a coffee table, and end tables to hold a drink or reading glasses. Here, the sofa and chairs don't "match" per se, but they do complement each other through their blue-and-white palette. Some of the pieces even mix patterns: the Louis XIII–style armchair (above) has a floral face and a traditional check backing.

THE LIVING ROOM

Anything and everything happens in the living room of a winter house, day or night. One person sits back with a cup of cocoa and pores over a selection of books. Another takes a nap underneath a toasty throw. A tray of après-ski drinks is set out on a tray for all to enjoy while watching the snow fall. The whole gang takes in a movie or challenges one another to a ruthless Scrabble tournament. If you're lucky, there's a fireplace where guests can pull up a chair and warm their toes.

At our place, the living room is the first real room you enter. A pair of portieres separates this room from the foyer, giving the transition between the two spaces definition and drama. The portieres not only add a touch of softness and color but also shield the living room against wintry blasts of air from the front door. Both sides of the portieres can be seen, so I made the front and back from two different blue paisley fabrics—one ground is pale, the other dark—that give each space a distinct identity.

It's a quirky room with a great double-height ceiling that echoes the loftiness of the nearby mountains, and big windows frame the glorious view. When you walk in, you feel as if you just took a deep breath outdoors, although you're obviously protected inside. The height of the living area was one of the things that sold me from the start. I loved the light, the view through the tall French doors, and the sense of ease the expansive space created. Still, a tall room like this one also posed a decorating challenge, since ordinary furnishings are easily dwarfed. The solution is to fool your eye into regularizing the

"The joy of a house is to be in it as much as possible."

FRANÇOISE DE LA RENTA

Interaction with nature is an underlying inspiration in this room, from the Audubon prints framing the window and the Aubusson pastoral scene set into a velvet pillow on the sofa (both opposite) to the antique faience jardiniere (above) painted with a gardening theme.

scale. The dark wood beams of the ceiling visually stop your gaze from floating toward the sky. Large hanging lanterns reach down into the room, while tall cabinets reach upward, integrating the vertical space. The tall windows are softened by long curtains and balanced by large Audubon prints "stacked" in pairs on the walls alongside. These images seem a little like windows themselves, looking out onto their own landscape. The result is a space that feels unified and warm despite its unusually high ceilings.

I had never done a room for myself in a blue-and-white scheme before, but it all came together quickly. I had long coveted paisley panels in these colors from Clarence House, and when I saw the big windows in this room I knew the panels would be perfect for the curtains. They ended up driving the overall scheme, and a companion paisley was used for the sofa upholstery and the portieres. The dark wood beams and waxed stucco walls already in place when we bought the house were the perfect backdrop to the cool blue-and-white palette. Wood furnishings and a diamond-patterned sisal carpet add to the warmth.

The biggest requirement for a living room in any winter house is lots of seating, with the operating principle being that no matter where someone is in the room, he or she can be comfortable. If you have the space, you might wish to devise a main seating area for large groups as well as secondary groupings of furniture to accommodate splinter conversations or solitary readers. Varying chair sizes, shapes, and fabrics can ease the formality of the living room, as does the addition of plenty of ottomans and footstools for putting your feet up when you sit down. Because our living area has all of these essentials, the mood is relaxed, even though the house is full of antiques, and as a result this room is more like a family room than a formal sitting room. There is a large blue paisley sofa flanked by generously scaled chairs on either side of a coffee table. On one side, there is a French fauteuil upholstered in a soft blue-and-white woven fabric and edged in a delicate tape. On the other is a Louis XIII–style open armchair, covered in floral fabric and backed in the traditional manner with a check. Both chairs echo the room's blue-and-white color scheme, yet they're

A selection of rich fabrics adds depths to the upholstery and decorative pillows of a winter house. Clockwise from top left: a tapestry-style cut velvet covers a Bretagne bergere and ottoman; pillows of petit point framed by velvet and lush tassels; a vintage cable-knit sweater is reborn as a pillow cover; an Aubusson fragment and an ocelot muff find new life as pillows.

WINTER FABRICS

When you think of your wardrobe, you associate particular fabrics with specific seasons, such as crisp, colorful linen with summertime. Likewise, certain fabrics are right at home in a winter house. Their textures exude a feeling of warmth and comfort. Here are some of my favorites.

bouclé A nubby texture and hardy, substantial weight make it especially suitable for upholstery on small chairs, ottomans, footstools, and pillows.

cashmere Completely and utterly luxurious, it is perfect for winter-house throws and robes.

chenille Though some styles may need to be backed for strength, it is an excellent texture for upholstery—sitting on a chenille-covered chair or sofa feels like curling up in a big blanket—and good for pillows and throws, too.

embroidery If you choose the location for embroidery wisely and use it in thoughtful doses of luxury, it will truly be a standout; however, take care in its application, as threads can be pulled if used on high-traffic items such as chairs. It is more suitable for pillows, lamp shades, and headboards. Or go for broke (literally and figuratively!) and opt for embroidered curtains.

felt Good-quality, heavyweight wool, not your run-of-the-mill craft-project variety, is great for enormous table covers and curtains. You can use it unlined, lined, or double-backed.

flannel Cotton flannel sheets are a given in a winter house; you'll find them in all the linen mail-order catalogs. Wool flannels are suitable for upholstery, curtains, and wall treatments. Shop with a keen eye: I once found a sage green flannel at thirteen dollars per yard and made lined and interlined curtains for a room with fourteen-foot ceilings—the flannel was so soft it felt like cashmere.

knits Knits can't withstand a lot of tension and wear, so simple jerseys and luxurious sweater knits are best used for accents like pillows and throws instead of upholstery

matelasse Subtly textured, it makes beautiful bedcovers, shams, and tablecloths; mix with checks or provençal prints for casual contrast.

suede A genuine or man-made microfiber like Ultrasuede that can be washed is a good upholstery choice for ottomans and small chairs.

ticking stripe This faithful, durable, go-anywhere choice comes off the mattress and onto upholstered walls, curtains, and bedcovers. Use it all over, as you would toile.

velvet Even the name itself oozes richness. Not just for formal locations, it makes attractive bedcovers, curtains, and pillows. Choose cotton velvet over silk for a more casual look.

wool Look for a variety of patterns, such as houndstooth, herringbone, and plaid. Depending on the thickness, it can be used just about anywhere.

Note: Stroll through a local fabric shop and imagine the decorative possibilities of some of your favorite fashion fabrics: meltons for upholstery, silk organza for sheer curtains or lamp shade overlays, corduroy for an upholstered headboard.

quite different in style. A capacious French bergère that's so big you feel as if you're in your own world is paired with an ottoman that doesn't quite match—all the better, I say! I like a slight mismatch here and there to keep things from looking too "done" or decorated. A smaller sofa placed underneath the front window and set perpendicular to the larger paisley sofa is my husband's special place to read. When friends or family gather, it offers an extra spot for conversation—and there always seems to be more than one conversation going on in this house! The sofa visually anchors the large window, and its deep green upholstery adds richness and warmth to the room's blue-and-white scheme.

For comfort's sake, all throughout the living room are lots of cashmere or wool throws to snuggle under and small and large pillows in velvet, needlepoint, or Fortuny fabrics to prop behind you or to plunk down on the floor. Another thing you'll find everywhere is books, and these are just as vital for the mind and for the eye as throws and pillows are for the body. Books are among my favorite possessions, and they are an absolute necessity, because reading is a classic winter-house activity. It's important to have lots of inviting books and magazines readily available in the living room and elsewhere in the house so your guests never have to go far for something good to read. The coffee table is layered with books, and I place a rotating selection on a table behind the sofa for guests to choose from and take to their rooms as another way to make them feel at home. Books can also serve as an important decorating feature of a room: prop one on an easel and open it to a favorite image or place a tantalizing stack on a side table for someone to peruse. Just turn the page or rotate the books to create a very economical revolving art collection! Highlight a favorite artist, a seasonal theme, or a bit of local history. A magnifying glass placed beside your books encourages passersby to take a closer look.

books are

I love the idea of a rotating library—for my own use as well as for my guests'. A selection of books on a variety of topics awaits perusing on a narrow table behind the sofa. Natural horn (above and on the floral container opposite), as well as acorn and oak designs (as seen on a magnifying glass handle above) are recurring motifs throughout the house.

among my favorite possessions

I always hang a big garland of greens over the top and down the sides for fragrance.

Any home instantly takes on a wintry air indoors with a dressing of fresh greens. I use clippings and garlands of evergreen, fir, juniper, and eucalyptus in abundance whenever I can. While beautiful to look at, the fragrance alone suggests winter. A large-scale eighteenth-century French mantel with a royal crest frames the fireplace.

Those who know me well might be surprised to find a television in my living room. Sharing a good movie over a huge bowl of popcorn is practically an inalienable right in a winter house, and since this is the main gathering spot, I acquiesced. Truth be told, this one came with the house, so I just kept it there and tucked it away in an armoire-like cabinet. But the television isn't the focal point of the room. For me, the best place to be is in front of the fire. A winter house without a fireplace is, with all due respect to Coco Chanel, like "a button without a buttonhole." Encourage interaction by placing small chairs near the hearth to invite guests to perch close to the fire. The flames have a truly mesmerizing effect. Some of your best winter-house conversations will happen while you're sitting fireside, watching the flickering light. Create a holiday display on the mantel above by hanging a stocking or two, arranging a selection of greeting cards, or standing a large vase of greenery. Our mantel is a bit too shallow for such a tableau, but I always hang a big garland of greens over the top and down the sides for fragrance. Sitting on the sofa reading on a chilly day with the scent of evergreens around me is a winter treat I will always associate with my grandmother's house, the front door of which was surrounded by yew trees and other evergreens. That wonderful fragrance was distinctive of my grandmother's house.

For a final touch, carefully position small flower arrangements around the room to add scent and color that evoke varying moods. Though this is an easy and affordable pleasure year-round, it is especially welcome in winter, when it is least expected. You don't need to use fancy urns or lots of different flowers to achieve a great effect. Think outside the vase and consider your own inventive containers: I purchased a Black Forest inkstand for the charm of its animal carvings but ultimately used it to hold small arrangements. Any number of containers, from juice glasses to plastic bottles, can be used as liners inside your vases to convert and protect them.

This softly patterned scheme has a little bit of everything, including florals, chenille trims, paisley, and a houndstooth check. This makes it a versatile choice for a public space meant to service several different people, such as a family room, great room, or foyer. Every pattern is softened, and there is great opportunity for contrast. The traditional wools and plaid would be beautiful on large-scale pieces of furniture. The wood-grain wall-paper (top center) can be used on walls and ceilings where architecture of note is lacking.

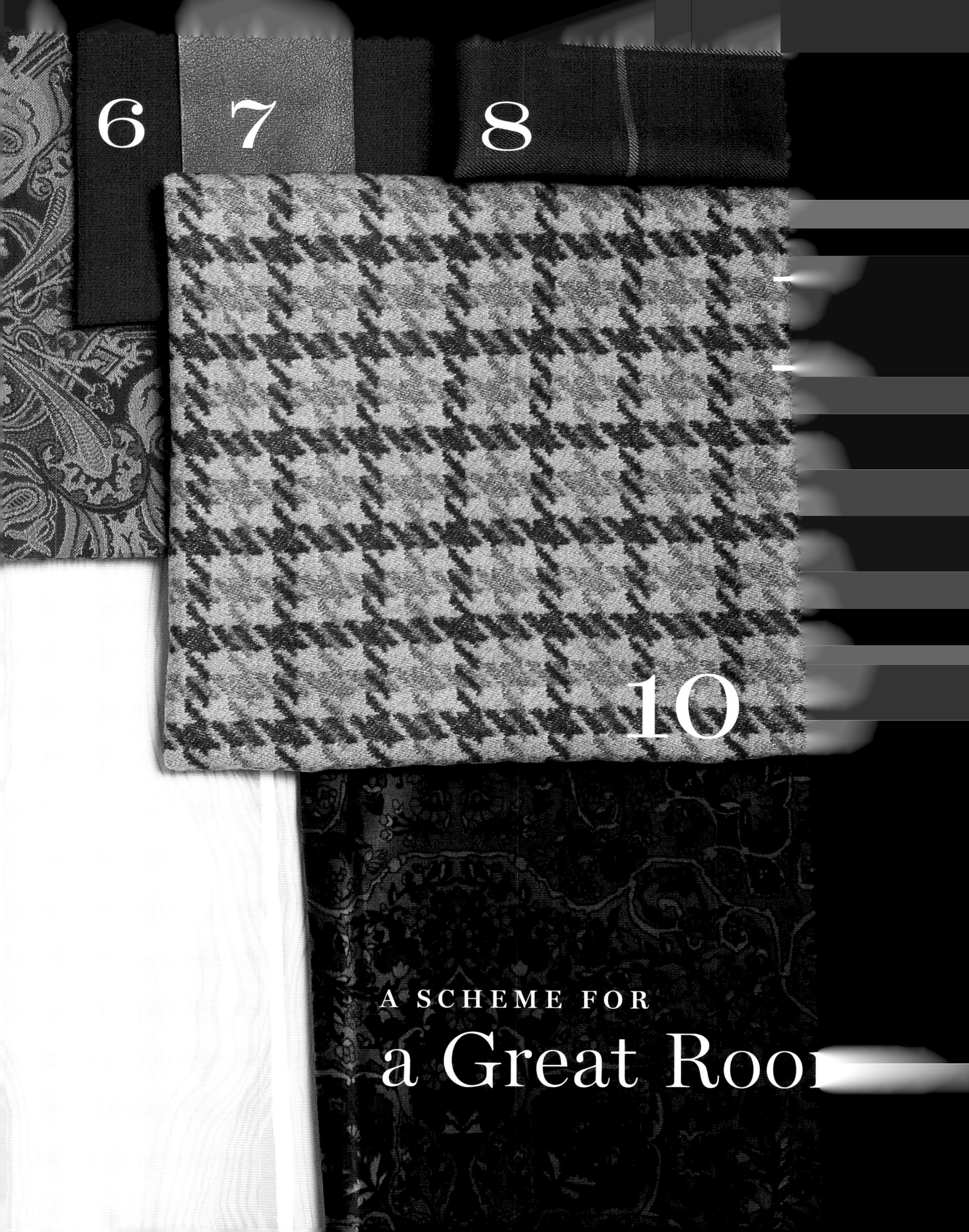

6 7 8

10

A SCHEME FOR

a Great Roo

"Flowers, food, fragrances—these aspects of housekeeping, ephemeral though they may seem, are vital parts of a whole, chic household."

Mark Hampton

THE DINING AREA

Almost any meal is a cause for celebration in a winter house. Of course, there are the holiday heavies like Thanksgiving, Christmas, and New Year's Eve. But there are also more intimate dinners and luncheons to salute the gathering of old friends or to mark the return of a skier with a healed injury to the slopes. A breakfast might feature the signature dish of a "guest chef" (at my house, it's the famous silver-dollar pancakes made by my husband, Barry). The dining area is also the scene for leisurely rituals like afternoon tea, a warm sherry, or evening cocktails. Large or small, these gatherings say so much about the hospitality of our homes and contribute to the warmth of time spent in a winter house.

Our main living space is visually divided into the living room and the dining area. Though there's no physical barrier between the two, the dining area feels very much like its own distinct space. When we entertain, guests—and conversation—flow naturally from one end to the other. The twelve-foot-long, refectory-style antique chestnut table is placed perpendicular to the paisley sofa, and ten chairs are upholstered in vicuña-colored suede. All of our meals—with the exception of casual bites sometimes taken in the kitchen or out on the terrace après ski—happen here. The table bisects the room, and hung high on the walls at either end are a large painting and a mirror to further define the space. The mountainside houses in the painting call to mind the view of Aspen Mountain that can be seen through the windows of the living room, so it's no surprise I was drawn to it the moment I saw it. Beneath the painting is a marble-topped Irish pine sideboard. An antique pine cabinet set against the wall does double duty, providing both storage and visual interest. I enjoy seeing some of my favorite things through the cabinet's windowed doors rather than hiding them away. In between uses, tureens, chargers, cachepots, candlesticks, and silver pieces make a wonderful display.

To accommodate the ever-changing numbers of diners in a winter house, I recommend buying the biggest table that sits comfortably in your space. At the dining table you can experiment with wintry motifs through your choice of china, linens, flatware, and flowers.

THE KITCHEN

Good things come from the kitchen of a winter house: crowd-pleasing roasts, hearty one-pot meals (my favorite), delicious desserts. This simple, stick-to-your-ribs fare helps recharge the soul. Fragrant herbs and spices mingle to fill the air with a comforting scent. The kitchen is often bustling with activity—everyone passes through during the day for a snack or to warm up with a hot drink. It's a good idea to have a lot of mugs on hand for teas, herbal infusions, cocoa, coffee, or your poison of choice.

The long galley kitchen of our Aspen house is really an extension of the living and dining areas, and it shares the same waxed stucco walls and paisley curtains. As befits a working space, the materials used here are more practical: a slate floor, dark-stained wood cabinets, butcher-block surfaces, and green marble around the deep farmhouse sink. A large island consisting of a low center unit with a long planter flanked by tall cabinets at each end separates the kitchen from the dining area. The walnut planter is lined with blue-and-white delft tiles; when filled with foliage or flowers it helps screen the kitchen from the dining area. Sometimes it is massed with herbs like lavender or rosemary, which can be used for cooking, infusions, or just a pinch of wonderful scent. I'll never forget the first time I saw a huge hedge of rosemary. I was in the south of France, and I found it intoxicating. This planter is a small reminder of that experience, and I just love having something alive, green, and fragrant growing indoors when it's cold outside. For a more adaptable design, I hung a blue paisley café curtain between the tall cabinets. When the curtain is open, I can toss a salad in the kitchen while chatting with my husband or family in the living room. For more formal occasions, I pull the curtain shut, making the kitchen invisible from the dining table.

en **bustling** with activity

LITTLE LUXURIES

THE TEA TRAY

When it comes to tea, I stand by the Boy Scout motto "Be prepared." I believe guests feel most comfortable when they can be self-sufficient and enjoy a drink or a snack without having to rummage around or bother the host. In other words, they should feel *at home.* A fully stocked tea tray is always in our kitchen, ready for anyone at any time. As a Zen master might say, "The ease of doing things leads to greater pleasure."

tea Stock a variety of caffeinated and noncaffeinated teas and herbal infusions to enjoy at breakfast, in the afternoon, and before bedtime. Some of my favorite blends—imperial jasmine, violet, and vanilla—come from Mariage Frères in Paris; I always tuck a few tins in my bag when I come home from a trip.

teapots and teacups My china-collecting gene dictates that I not neglect teapots! For me, every antique teapot tells a story. Guests enjoy picking "their pot" from an eclectic collection and bringing it to their rooms. Often I will preselect a set and a tray for each guest room for some decorating on a small scale. Your cups, pots, and serving pieces need not match; a bit of a mix makes individual teatime all the more interesting.

accessories Dress your tea tray with an antique or embroidered linen, a mix of silverware, a sugar bowl and creamer of crystal or pressed glass, a tea strainer for loose teas, a vase with a fresh flower or two, a small tin of tea biscuits, a plate of fresh fruit, or something freshly baked.

Potted herbs such as rosemary are attractive, fragrant, and useful. As a reminder of nature's sleeping beauty outdoors, they also perfume the air, and you can snip off a few sprigs when cooking or to prepare an infusion of tea. Here a hedge of rosemary is created in this antique walnut planter inset with Delft tiles depicting miniature landscapes of far-off places.

Public Areas

Not every nook and cranny of a winter house is explored by all, but there are two places in particular that everyone sees and uses, and very often they are the most overlooked when it comes to their decor.

Hallways are ideal spaces for displaying a few of your favorite things. In mine you'll find a traditional—and thankfully cuckoo-less—Black Forest–style clock (above) and a framed Hermès scarf depicting French châteaux (opposite).

HALLWAYS AND STAIRWELLS

A winter house is a high-traffic zone. Because somebody is always coming or going, upstairs or downstairs or back and forth through the halls, I find that practical, hard-working materials like slate, limestone, sisal carpet, and antique wood on the floors can best handle lots of abuse from luggage, ski boots, and canine feet. But don't look at hallways and stairwells with just a utilitarian eye. These areas of a winter house should reflect the same sense of warmth and welcome your guests felt when they entered your front door.

I tend to opt for maximum visual impact. Many paintings and etchings of landscapes and natural settings or outdoor activities are found on the walls throughout my house, but there are lots of alternatives to traditional artwork. Hallway walls are a great canvas for exhibiting various collections, and the things you choose to display can reinforce a winter motif. For example, the stairwell that leads to the lower level of my house and the hallways beyond is lined with reproductions of vintage ski posters. The colors are bold, and winter themes such as tumbling skiers, ski fashionistas, and horse-drawn sleds are entertaining. Placed near the stairs and coat closet, a clock gives both guests and family a convenient place to check the time on their way in or out. Images of your special interests speak volumes to your guests. A reproduction series of Turgot's map of Paris—one of my own favorite places—hangs on the second-floor landing. Though printed in individual plates, when framed tightly together they all read as one continuous landscape.

CHÂTEAUX HISTORIQUES DE LA FRANCE
An 1852
1 Château d'Hyères
2 de Joux
3 La Tour de Roussillon
4 de la Rouquette
5 du Mt. St Michel
6 de Beaurevoir
7 de Montlery
8 de Falaise
9 Château-Bayard
10 de Polignac
11 Château-Gaillard
12 de Niort
13 d'Etampes
14 de Vigny
15 de Créqui
16 d'Angoulême
17 de Pierrefonds
18 de Foix
19 de Vendôme
20 Vieux-Louvre
21 de Coucy
22 de Frasmes
23 de Montargis
24 Tour de Rouen
25 de Rosny
26 d'Harcourt
27 de Valencay
28 de Carcassonne
29 Tour de Mt Royan
30 de La Queue
31 de Barbe-Bleue
32 de Tancarville
33 de Gisors
34 de Brie Comte Rob.
35 des Tuileries
36 de la Rochefoucault
37 de Plessis-les Tours
38 de Tarascon
39 de Ham
40 de la Roche-Guyon
41 de Maintenon
42 de Tournœlles
43 Château de Pau
44 d'Amboise
45 de Boussac
46 de Blaye
47 de Chatillon
48 du Temple
49 de Luzarches
50 de Pornic
51 de Couches
52 de la Brèdes
53 de Chambord
54 de la Malmaison
55 de Sully
56 de Vincennes
57 de Randon
58 de Fontainebleau
59 de Versailles
60 de St. Cloud
61 d'Anet
62 Chenonceaux
63 de la Bastille
64 de St. Germain
65 d'Azay-le-Rideau
66 de Clisson
HERMÈS-Paris

Images of your special speak

You might consider a hallway your own personal gallery space. Grouping like or related images, such as my Turgot's map of Paris here and the vintage ski travel posters on the following pages, in the same style of frames unifies the group.

interests
volumes to your guests.

DOLOMITI E ALPI ORIENTALI

CORTINA D'AMPEZZO

ALTIP. DI ASIAGO - VAL GARDENA - COLLE ISARCO - SAN MARTINO DI CASTROZ
VIPITENO - AVELENGO (MERANO) - MENDOLA - TARVISIO - MADONNA DI CAMPIGLI
COLLALBO SUL RENON (BOLZANO) - MISURINA

ALPI OCCIDENTALI

CLAVIÈRES - COURMAYEUR - BARDONECCHIA
LIMONE PIEMONTE - SAUZE D'OULX - CESANA - OROPA

SPORTS D'HIVER
ANS LES
ARAVIS
AUTE SAVOIE
AC D'ANNECY
VALLEE DE THÔNES
ACLUSAZ-G^D BORNAND
PLM
a. maeght

POWDER ROOMS

Powder rooms may be small in square footage, but they can—and should—have a big impact. Shared by guests, powder rooms offer yet another way to entertain or charm them. If you have fun, everyone will enjoy his or her visit! (Legendary style makers Nancy Lancaster and Elsie de Wolfe always decorated bathrooms as if they were living areas, complete with furniture and artwork. Makes sense, no?) I also think they are the perfect places to try a new decorating style. Sometimes it's a lot easier to experiment in powder rooms; after all, they are only visited for a few moments. If you're brave enough to try out bold designs in these small rooms, that kick-in-the-pants courage may enable you to take more risks in larger spaces.

The powder rooms in my Aspen house echo the themes of the living area, yet each has a distinct mood and style all its own. I make sure each is stocked with a fragrant candle, a fresh bouquet, soap in a silver basket, and embroidered linen hand towels to welcome my guests. Artwork and collections are also at home on the walls of these diminutive spaces. I collect vintage *Vogue* magazines, so in one powder room I framed photocopies of covers from the forties and fifties and grouped them on the wall. I chose covers with a graphic appeal and winter themes in the hope that their reminder of yesterday's sports and styles would make my guests smile. In another powder room, a tiny painting portrays a man, a cart, and a road that leads who knows where, and watercolors from a nineteenth-century traveling sketchbook depict European views. I'm not a painter myself, but as a diligent keeper of notebooks and journals, I can appreciate the efforts made by the sketch artist.

The guest powder room on the main floor is covered in a rich paisley wallpaper incorporating the color of the marble vanity and sink. A growing collection of small paintings and watercolors decorate the walls and are reflected in an antique gilt French mirror.

"There, all is order and beauty, richness, quiet and pleasure."

CHARLES BAUDELAIRE

H

HOMEWORK

THE NECESSARY—AND UBIQUITOUS— WASTEPAPER BASKET

While wastepaper baskets might not be as essential as air and water, they are something we all need. As I see it, the issue is how to make this necessity attractive and integrate it into your decor rather than have it scream at you every time you enter the room.

decorative techniques I prefer decorative wastepaper baskets that complement and disappear into the room. The most simple option is to cover a wastepaper basket in fabric or wallpaper to match your walls. Wire or woven baskets can blend in with a lining of matching fabric. If you're feeling especially creative, try collage or decoupage, or even hand-paint a design; of course, you could also commission someone to do this for you.

alternatives Some of the best wastepaper baskets I've seen aren't wastepaper baskets at all but repurposed containers that do the job beautifully. Depending on the style and needs of your room, toss your papers into a jardiniere, an overscale cachepot, or a galvanized bucket. Just like a cheap lamp shade, a bad wastepaper basket is guaranteed to draw attention and diminish your design.

etiquette I don't think there is a documented etiquette when it comes to wastepaper baskets, so I will take this opportunity to issue my own. First and foremost, it is a design travesty to take an otherwise attractive wastepaper basket and insert a plastic bag into it with the edges folded over the sides. Please don't do this. If you feel an undeniable urge to line your basket with something, place a paper doily in the bottom, which can be tossed away when the basket is full and replaced. This is one of my (many) decorating pet peeves. Remember, your home is not a budget motel.

A Space of

One's Own

“Ah, there is nothing like staying home for real comfort.”

Jane Austen

2

A Space of One's Own

PRIVATE QUARTERS GUEST RETREATS

Every house, of course, is a mix of public and private spaces. The rooms in the previous chapter—the living room, dining area, and kitchen—are some of the places where we gather for a meal or conversation. But all houses also need quiet spots where you can get away from everything and everyone for some time on your own. Depending on your home, hobbies, and habits, this retreat might be a separate room, such as a study, or simply a corner in an existing room that your family agrees is "yours." It's not the physical configuration that matters, but the feeling created there. This retreat should be yours alone—or, at the very least, you should feel as if it is!

When guests are staying with you, they should be able to enjoy not just the pleasure of your company but also their own private moments of rest and relaxation. The trick is to make your visitors feel at home while providing a sense of privacy and freedom. By at home, I mean they should be comfortable enough to come and go as they please for activities and meals and actually use the rooms as if they were made just for them. You can make guests feel special in their own spaces through your decoration, linens, accessories, and thoughtful extra touches. Aim for a feeling of comfort and the ability to transport guests both physically and mentally to another place for the duration of their stay.

With the clubhouse atmosphere and community spirit in a winter house—at meals, on the slopes, playing games—both you and your guests must have places reserved for personal time. These private spaces are most often found in bedrooms and bath areas.

Private Quarters

Anyone who comes to stay with us in Aspen more or less has free rein of the whole house. It's that old "ma maison est votre maison" *philosophy. Although there are lots of places in our home to which I can retreat, such as my favorite chair in the living room or the banquette in the mud/flower room at the back of the house, my most comforting and personal escape is our bedroom and bath. The bedroom is more than just a place to sleep: it is where I like to read, write letters, take a phone call, and simply collect my wits! And the bath is a great place for relaxation and contemplation: I can take a long, fragrant soak in the tub while listening to a favorite CD.*

An antique French inkwell, one of my favorite items in the house, now serves as a desk organizer for pens and glasses; paper clips are stored in compartments.

THE MASTER BEDROOM

Our bedroom is on the first floor just off the main hallway, which makes it close to a lot of the activity of the house, yet it remains private. And that's what makes it all the more cozy once you step inside and close the door. If a winter house is a nest for the winter, then this bedroom is the nest within the nest.

And in this nest within a nest (are you with me?), there is *another* nest—the bed. Our bedroom is not huge, and when you enter, your attention is immediately drawn to the canopied bed. One of the first pieces of furniture I envisioned here, it is one of my favorites. I always record decorating ideas and inspirations the moment I find them so that the schemes for rooms using these concepts can come together quickly later. The inspiration for this bed came from my travels: I had slept in a similar one at Château Bagnols in France. Our Aspen bedroom offered the perfect setting for a classic *lit à la polonaise;* with the canopy above and the headboard and footboard at the same height, you really feel as if someone has tucked you in (whether you have been or not!). Its sense of protection and enclosure calls to mind childhood pleasures like sleeping in a tent or hanging out in a fort made of blankets. In the winter, it feels warm and cozy; when we visit in the summer, it is cool and shady.

The decorating scheme came together with great ease. Several years ago, I had tucked away in my basket of

VOGUE
HEALTHY ESCAPES
TRAVEL

I love this sense of envelopment

"fabric favorites" a swatch of Pierre Frey French cotton fabric; its deep celery ground punctuated by pinks, reds, tobacco, and violet gave it a somewhat autumnal feeling in tune with the rest of the house. It was floral but not too feminine for our bedroom. (I am very lucky to have a husband who loves what I do and doesn't second-guess me when it comes to decorating. He is always as pleased with the results as I am.) The fabric also worked well with the soft celery green already on the walls when we bought the house, so in an uncanny way the scene was already set, as if this bedroom had been waiting for me and this bed.

In the traditional French style, the bed hangings, curtains, and upholstery are all treated in a single printed fabric. I love this sense of envelopment, and the flowers of the print make me feel as though we're deep in a garden even when snow is falling outside. Contrasting pattern is added through a layering of smaller elements: antique silk tiebacks, a needlepoint bellpull, and a mix of antique and new pillows on the bed. It's a serene space that has all the practical essentials—books, light to read by, a fresh carafe of water, and scented candles and flowers.

You want to spend more time in a bed like this for a long read or breakfast (sometimes more a fantasy than a reality). The bedside table is indispensable for holding books, a carafe of water or a pot of tea, or any number of essentials. My husband's bedside table holds a good reading lamp, a miniature trunk full of his "stuff," a framed watercolor propped against the wall, a clock, and a nighttime tray. The trunk keeps miscellany like pens and reading glasses hidden but accessible for midnight brainstorms. There is a layering of textures—the fabric insert on the fruitwood table, the tole lamp with its soft silk shade, the brass

"Something old, something new" best describes this combination (right) of antique tassels with a new fabric.

LITTLE LUXURIES

THE BED TRAY

Since one of the goals of a winter house (or any house) should be to encourage some relaxation, it is only natural to make the bed tray a prominent fixture of your nest. What could be more relaxing than getting lost in a book, writing in a journal, or having a snack in the comfort of your own bed? The very suggestion of a bed tray is rather luxurious; even if you could do the same activity without the tray, its presence adds a bit of ceremony and pampering to the occasion. For me, a bed tray symbolizes one of the ultimate fantasies: having enough time in the morning to read and reflect before the demands of the day begin. A leisurely cup of coffee in bed is a treat I try to give myself whenever I can, but wouldn't we all love more time to use a bed tray! To encourage such wanton behavior, I tuck these trays under the beds or in the closets of many rooms in our Aspen home.

styles Bed trays can be found in wicker, bamboo, wood, and lacquer, in a range of styles from traditional to crisply modern. The ideal tray satisfies your eye and is practical: large enough to accommodate a full place setting, sturdy enough to hold hot beverages without wobbling, and designed to fold flat for storage if you're short on space. Storage compartments come in handy; if you are like me you probably have several books as well as newspapers, magazines, mail-order catalogs, and letters tucked in the pockets and awaiting attention. Sounds like a portable desk, doesn't it? That's the great thing about a bed tray—the options are endless.

setting According to Henry James, "summer evening" are two of the sweetest words in the English language. That's nice, but "room service" works for me! When using a bed tray for a meal, you should feel as though you're having room service at home. Use a mix of your favorite china and linens to set your tray, and add a small flower arrangement or just a single bud in a vase whenever possible.

occasions Breakfast in bed is the classic scenario, but it isn't the only reason to use a bed tray. Spend a Sunday morning with the newspaper spread out and read it cover to cover, curl up with a pot of tea and a book on a rainy day, bring your spouse or a guest an afternoon snack, or serve yourself a light supper in bed on a night when you're home alone. As my often-quoted friend Kinsey Marable says, complete with southern (Virginia, that is) drawl, "There's nothing bettah than a tray suppah." Amen!

A painting can act as an extra window in a room. In this particular work, I was drawn to the tree and its bench with the subliminal message "Come have a seat."

clock, the velvet and walnut box—that was done subconsciously but is in keeping with the concept of textures throughout the rest of the house. My own bedside table has a tole reading lamp to match my husband's, as well as a few must-haves like fresh flowers and a water carafe, heavy-duty moisturizer, and lip balm to battle the effects of the dry air and altitude. Also on my nightstand are personal items such as a violet shagreen photo frame with family photos; depending on my mood, these and other objects often rotate with similar items on a bookcase opposite the bed.

The settee at the end of the bed was a practical consideration; it's a place to pause, put on shoes, or rest when returning from town with packages or a handbag. Most important, it serves as a perch for my dogs when they come for a visit. An antique chair upholstered in the same fabric as many of the other pieces in the room offers a resting spot for taking phone calls. I use a simple painted French table as a desk where I open mail, review phone messages, and store stationery. I spend time at this desk on personal projects like writing in my journals or updating my scrapbooks and try to perform only social tasks such as writing thank-you notes here; I really believe that you should avoid doing work in the bedroom, particularly in a winter house, where the goal is to rest and relax!

There is a fireplace in our bedroom. It is gas, not woodburning (as are all the fireplaces in new houses in Aspen). And although you don't get that wonderful, wintry scent of burning logs, it takes the edge off the cold and is a great way to warm up upon waking or after a bath. Even with the heat or, perhaps more accurately, in spite of it, I always keep a window cracked a bit when sleeping. I guess it's also the southerner in me—though the crickets are all buried under two feet of snow, I like to think I'd hear them if I could!

Bedside tables are multitaskers. With necessities such as alarm clocks and water carafes close at hand they also beg for some decoration with favorite items like the drawings and miniature paintings that I have seated here.

on my mood,
objects often rotate

Beyond the usual decorating concerns of palette, fabric, upholstery, and window coverings, I choose antiques and artwork to further infuse a room with personality and interest. As a lover of antiques, I forgive their quirks and eccentricities. For example, an antique French clock with gilt highlights was built in above the fireplace and painted in hues similar to those of the walls. It keeps time erratically, according to its mood, but that only adds to its charm. On the desk sits an inkstand I couldn't resist when I saw it. Wheat, flowers, fruit, a beehive, and gardening tools form the decoration. It reminds me of summertime pleasures even on the coldest days. Antiques like this stand may not seem functional at first glance but are surprisingly easy to adapt to modern purposes. The compartments hide paper clips; the tray is used to store pens and reading glasses.

A few paintings hang in the bedroom, and like so much of the artwork in the house their theme is inspired by winter, nature, and seasonal activities. A small oil depicts ice-skaters and a romantic image of a warmly bundled-up gentleman pushing madame (or is it mademoiselle?), whose only protection from the cold is an elegant dress and a tiny muff, on a sled. I am drawn to images of people enjoying themselves. The English painting of a tree immediately drew me in when I first saw it. Was it the strength of the large tree, the inviting bench, or the combination? It doesn't really matter. What is important is the connection one feels with art or an object. If your own wall space is limited, display artwork or framed pictures on stands or easels placed on tables, atop chests, or in bookcases. It's a great way to feature smaller pieces and fill in awkward spaces such as those around table lamps.

H

HOMEWORK

LAYERED LOOKS

Winter's cold encourages layering, both for our bodies, whether we are on or off the ski slopes, and for our homes. From a decorator's point of view, layering allows for an interplay of texture and pattern. You can exercise this concept in several venues:

on the floor Layer floor coverings to create welcome warmth. For example, place a needlepoint or kilim rug on top of a neutral diamond-patterned sisal in a bedroom. The sisal unifies the colors of the room, while the needlepoint or kilim adds brightness, visually anchors the bed, and provides a soft, warm landing place for that first foot out of the covers on a wintry morning. In the summer, you can pull up the area rugs and enjoy a simpler, crisper look. For centuries, this seasonal change was part of traditional decor. Whatever you choose to do, make sure that the base layer is always the quieter pattern; place the more "active" design on top.

on the dinner table The table affords multiple layering opportunities. You can layer two tartan or paisley throws over your main table covering, or put place mats on top of the textured grain of the table. Then layer a painted porcelain plate atop a wood charger or a simple porcelain plate on a silver charger, and layer further with a compatible or a contrasting soup bowl. Play with what you have, and experiment with low and high contrasts, patterned and plain dishes, colored and clear glassware.

on the bed You can layer either physically—a mattress topped by a feather bed topped by a sheet topped by a blanket topped by a duvet topped by a throw—or visually, with layers of mixed patterns of sheets and bed cover or accent pillows.

on the windows There are both aesthetic and practical concerns for layering on your windows. You can block out the cold and keep in the warmth with a shade covered by an undercurtain covered by a top curtain. Create contrast with fabric types and patterns. Be sensible: dress your windows appropriately; don't smother them.

"For me, true luxury is silence and space."
UNGARO

THE MASTER BATH

After a long day of travel or an active day of skiing, a leisurely, fragrant soak in the bath is bliss for the muscles and the mind. For me, a bath is a retreat in and of itself whether you choose to add Epsom salts, Mr. Bubble, or something more exotic to the water. And I can't think of a better place to partake of this ritual than in the deep, old-fashioned footed bathtub in our master bathroom. The tub came with the house, and its exterior is painted to resemble patinated copper, which emphasizes its antique look and helps it blend into the space around it. Overall, the master bath conveys a gardenlike feeling thanks to a wealth of flower motifs in the artwork and fabrics and the view of the outdoors. The bathtub sits in front of a bay window facing my "mini" grove of aspen trees in the front yard, which is enclosed by a high stone wall. Café curtains let in light and provide needed privacy, since this room and the master bedroom are at street level.

This room is one of my personal havens, and I must confess that I have stocked it with a veritable apothecary's worth of bathing accoutrements. A portable brass rack stretches across the tub and holds a pumice stone, a soft sea sponge, soap, and washcloths. A varied assortment of bath salts, oils, and lotions has been selected for their wonderful fragrances and abilities to soothe skin affected by icy air, drying heat, and altitude. I experiment with many different products, but I have favorites like Red Roses and Orange Blossom from my friend perfumer Jo Malone. Beside the tub a painted étagère stores other essentials, and a small chair stands nearby. Convenient cupboards are full of fluffy cotton towels and

While I feel subtle fragrance is important throughout a house, the bath can be your fragrance laboratory—a place to experiment with soaps, candles, and fresh flowers such as paperwhites, tuberose, or lavender.

hold my chenille robe. A selection of my favorite slippers—more-than-worn-in quilted cashmere slippers by Loro Piana and velvet mules by Manolo Blahnik and Stubbs & Wootten—are at the ready. My husband and I have our own sinks on opposite sides of the room; a door next to mine leads to a courtyard with a stone wall encircling the Jacuzzi where we sometimes spend some time with guests après ski.

When you have the space, select furnishings and accessories to transform a bath into a retreat that feels more like a true room. A chandelier and an Aubusson rug similar to others in the house finish our master bath and establish continuity. At the foot of the tub, a caned planter is massed with fragrant flowers that change with the seasons so there is something to look at while bathing. At different times during the year the planter is filled with orchids or hydrangeas for a wonderful shock of color, or I choose favorite blooms such as tuberose, paperwhite narcissus, and lavender for their scent. A few personal effects impart a sense of ownership. In the doorway leading to the master bedroom closet, a slipper chair holds a pillow given to me by my sister Cathy. Its whimsical motifs always make me laugh.

FOR MY DEAR...
SISTER

A SCHEME FOR
a Dining Room or
a Master Bedroom
1
2
3
4
5

This all-around scheme works in a public room as well as in a private room. Rich and textural, it is composed of velvets, paisleys, delicate florals, and a check. Depending on your selections, you could create a sense of movement or balance with light and dark fabrics and heavy and light textures. Make curtains from the embroidered fabric (bottom right), and add the small print (top right corner) as a surprising lining. Cover chairs in suede (left) and a sofa in paisley (lower left). The neutral striped floral (center right) makes a lovely upholstered desk chair.

Guest Retreats

I like to think that all the people passing in and out of our house help to keep it alive and happy. Some of my favorite memories are of times when our house is full for the holidays or everyone just comes together to have fun, like when a group of my girlfriends flew in for a big weekend-long pajama party. And I love listening to my nieces and nephews chattering away and one-upping each other's adventures as they recap a day of tackling the slopes and skiing the "double blacks." And while everybody enjoys these times together, the guest rooms provide a retreat for our friends and family where they can be self-sufficient while enjoying their private time.

When planning your guest rooms, ask yourself, "What would make my guests comfortable?" This might include a desk for writing and extra pillows for support while reading. Have you slept in your guest bedroom lately?

At the beginning of this chapter, I spoke about the importance of making guests feel special. Now, one of the basic tenets of being a host is that you generally don't invite people to your home unless you know them well. Since you do know your guests well, you understand their likes and dislikes, which enables you to prepare a retreat specifically tailored to each one. Space permitting, I try to have a comfortable chair or two and a footstool or ottoman in each room in addition to a bed, as well as a desk with plenty of pens and writing paper, postcards, and stamps. When it comes to decorating, guest rooms are one area where you should knock yourself out.

What makes guests feel indulged is not just the details but the overall look and feel of their personal space. Our house has three guest rooms on the upper level and one guest room and one guest apartment on the lower level. The rooms can accommodate different configurations of occupants: for example, one has a double bed for a couple, in another there are twin beds for siblings, friends, or an overflow of guests. We refer to each room by the name of its dominant color or pattern, and each has its own distinct personality driven by the decor.

One final word of advice before I take you on a tour of the guest rooms in my winter house: always spend at least one night yourself in each of your guest rooms. It's the only way to discover what works and what doesn't from the perspectives of both design and comfort.

A PROSPECT OF FLOWERS

THE GRAY ROOM

Sometimes a guest room calls out for a singular gesture that can compensate for its challenges. In the Gray Room, the challenge was size: it was originally a nanny's room and thus quite small. All that would fit in the room was a twin bed, so I wanted it to be a pretty spectacular example to make the room feel special. I chose an antique French bed and hung it with a generous canopy of a gray and cream ticking stripe; the same fabric is repeated at the windows. The scale of the bed hangings draws the eye upward so the room appears more spacious. The curtains on the windows are also in the same subtle stripe, and as a result the room seems wrapped in softness. The bed is positioned against the wall to maximize available floor space. High head- and footboards create a sleeping "envelope." Beside the bed, a tiered, painted table is capacious enough to hold a lamp, flowers, a water carafe, books, and a guest's miscellany. With the trellised wallpaper, an unusual gray and orange antique French quilt on the bed, and chairs upholstered in different fabrics, the room has quite a bit of pattern. Thanks to the soft tones, however, the patterns all peacefully coexist and the overall effect remains restful and serene.

I like to give my guests something to look at, and guest rooms are often an ideal place to display a collection. Two of my favorite themes are featured in this room. Images of fashionable women have long inspired me, and on the wall in the corner are six French engravings of elegant women framed simply in black. Everyone who knows me well is privy to my passion for chairs. With their open arms, they're the most hospitable piece of furniture in the house! I am fond of collecting miniature chairs—often antique samples from long-ago furniture makers or scaled-down seating once made for children or dolls. The miniature chairs in this room are a mix of French and English, new and old. Some come from my travels; others are special gifts. Placing them close together emphasizes their contrast of shapes, sizes, and textures—wood, fabric, rush, and caning. Almost any grouping of small objects can be displayed to its best advantage in this way; a group then becomes a collection.

Houses speak volumes. Therefore, every room —including the guest bedrooms—should express who you are. Curtain panels in a gray ticking fabric are trimmed with a ribbon that costs $5 per yard and actually looks like a fine petit point. The antique curtain tie-backs are French.

Fabrics in unexpected patterns or colors will engage the eye of your visitor. A single upholstered chair can wear an amusing design quite well. The small slipper chair near the window is one of my own designs, and its Clarence House fabric works a little like a Rorschach test: the white branches and dots reminded me of reindeer antlers and snowflakes when I chose it, but the pattern was actually inspired by the shapes of coral. I guess the lesson here is not to be afraid of using patterns that don't strictly fit into your scheme—if they are in a complementary palette they will usually work. Like several of the chairs in the living room, the French provincial chair has contrasting upholstery on the front (orange toile) and back (a tiny star and check design). I was mad for the orange toile when I first saw it; it was so unusual and ultimately fit in so well with this room. When you have a near-visceral response to a fabric, I recommend operating under the philosophy of "get it or you'll regret it"—you might never encounter it again and even if you don't have an immediate use for it, if you really love it you'll eventually find a place for it. Living proof of this theorem is the fact that I have never seen another toile in that same lively hue!

In the adjoining bath, a silver tray on the counter holds a soap dish and ceramics in shades of gray to house bath necessities; a silver cup of flowers adds a splash of bright color and says "welcome" to a guest. Small bouquets can be arranged in cups, bud vases, or other petite containers. Remember, gestures like these can have a surprisingly big impact.

The lively and unusual orange toile fabric on the face of this French chair (opposite) adds a splash of color to the otherwise pale gray color scheme.

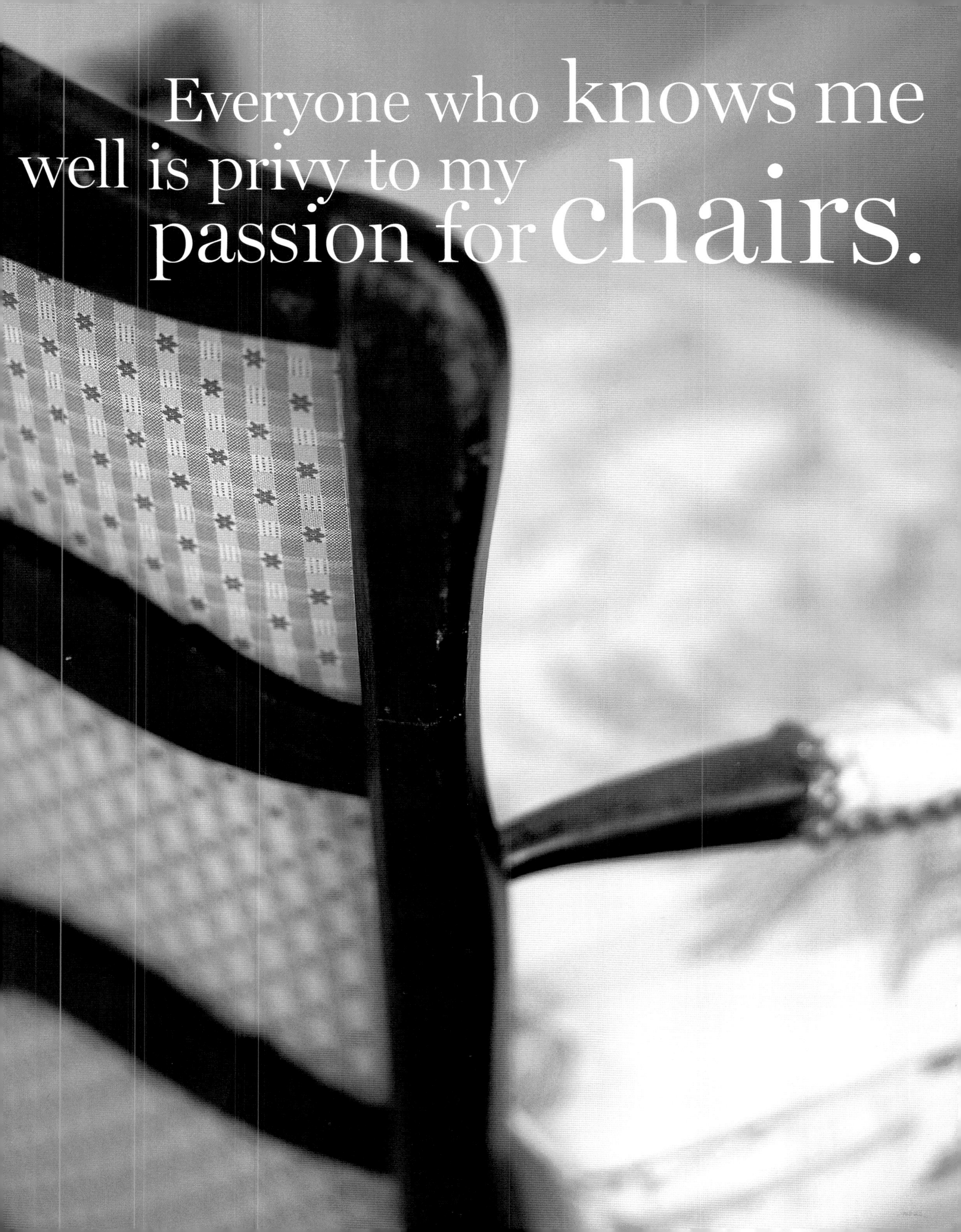

Everyone who knows me well is privy to my passion for chairs.

THE PINK ROOM

I wanted one of the guest rooms in this house to be in a soft and feminine palette. I chose this fabric from Manuel Canovas because of its subtle motif—squirrels sitting on tree branches. The surprisingly springlike palette of clear pinks accented by periwinkle blues and butter yellows accomplishes the feminine goal. Combined with romantic floral motifs, the soft palette creates a retreat that's reminiscent of warm-weather pleasures. Not every room in a winter house needs to fit so stringently into a predictable wintry frame of mind!

A subtle sense of humor is a must for rooms I design. With their tasseled tiebacks, the periwinkle curtains at the windows are dressy but their whimsical squirrel motif makes them seem more playful and less serious than a traditional damask would feel. Crystal bead trim was added along the inner edge of the curtains. The crystal beads gleam like ice melting in the sun as a nod to what is going on in the world outdoors. I love the way they catch the light. Window jewelry? Perhaps, or just a little indulgence. Thoughtful details like these help define the personality and style of a space.

While looking for a queen-size bed for this room, I came across this Louis XV–style model. I admired the shape of its headboard and finials, and as with the bed in the master bedroom the headboard and footboard here are the same height and hug the sleeper with that "tucked in" feeling. The bed linens are embroidered with pink patterns and topped by an antique chintz quilt and a pink velvet bedspread, as well as some Aubusson and needlepoint pillows. More fashionable engraved ladies from my collection grace the wall above the headboard. Every room needs lighting that fits seamlessly into the environment, and the bedside lamp with the floral-bedecked porcelain base and ruffled shade perfectly fits the room's feminine mood. It is also tall enough to provide good light for bedtime reading.

This is one of the larger guest rooms in the house and had the capacity for the additional seating provided by a settee. Nestled in between two built-in closets, it becomes a cozy spot where two people might pause for some conversation or someone might settle in alone with a newspaper and a cup of coffee before the day begins. A soft paisley throw adds comfort on chilly afternoons.

I wanted one room in a feminine palette.

In addition to the palette, the details are what make this the perfect room for a lady—French fashion plates above the headboard, butterflies on the tea set, and flowers on the porcelain lamp base.

THE TOILE ROOM

If you have more than one guest room, it's a practical move to set them up differently to house various arrangements of guests. I planned on placing twin beds in one of the guest rooms of this house for a little flexibility. Unlike most of the others, this cozy room with a dormered ceiling at the top of the stairs had a wide expanse of wall so there was plenty of space for a pair of headboards and a chest of drawers in between. The beds and the wall brackets and mirror frame above them are all nineteenth-century faux bamboo. I've always liked this look and have used it for many of my clients' homes, whether they are in Palm Beach, California, or Aspen. When I found this pair of beds I was finally able to translate the look to my own home. A black-and-white toile fabric by Brunschwig & Fils dominates the room. The caramel-colored tone of the wooden beds warms the room and prevents it from feeling too stark.

You might notice that this isn't the only room in the house where a single fabric is used in various ways throughout a room. There's a method to the madness: repetitions of fabric create a calm and soothing effect. In this room, the light-ground black-and-white toile is repeated on the walls, the windows, the dust ruffles on the beds, and even the ceiling, to emphasize its appealing shape. The toile continues into the bath, where it is used on the windows and the shower curtain. I hoped that guests, enveloped in pattern, might feel as though they were sleeping under the eaves in an alpine chalet or lodge. This toile is a somewhat unusual example. Instead of being a dense depiction of a pastoral or battle scene as is common with most toile fabrics, it has a lighter feel, with disparate elements such as follies, fruit, insects, and animals. It established a nice, clean patterned backdrop for the assorted components of the room. I have to admit, working with a black-and-white palette was so easy and neutral, and it was a

"Extending an invitation is to assume responsibility for another's happiness the entire time spent under one's roof."

ANTHELME BRILLAT-SAVARIN

The Hyson Extra
OPIUM

I look for pieces that inspire conversation

departure for me not to have to think about a color scheme! I did elect to punch things up a bit with deep reds and other dark, rich colors via the paisley duvets and unmatched (yet complementary) throws on the beds and the upholstery fabric on the reading chair. The floor was layered with a needlepoint carpet on top of a basketweave wool carpet in deep camel. These rich tones also contributed to the more alpine feel of this room, which is further emphasized by framed engravings of chalets and rustic French farmhouses.

The room is equipped with some of the usual suspects to make it feel like home. The window embrasure is just large enough to fit a desk and a chair. Desks are usually a part of all of the bedrooms I decorate for my own homes and those of my clients. My friends and family are readers and writers like I am, so I make sure there is a comfortable place where they can jot down a note, hook up a laptop, or just pile up their magazines and books. Desktops also serve as the perfect place to set flowers, candles, and, when not otherwise in use, a tea or break-

This room is all about the mix—faux bamboo, the lightness of toile wallpaper, the saturation of paisleys and velvet, and the juxtaposition of the Chinese tea tin and engravings of chalets.

fast tray. In my view, it is essential for guests to have a surface on which they can enjoy a private meal. This desk is accompanied by a rustic French rush-bottomed chair with a small floral pillow for comfort. Other furnishings include a comfortable French chair with an ottoman and a good floor lamp in the corner to give guests a private place to curl up and read or simply put up their feet for a spell.

If you are the type to invite your guests to come and stay for an extended period of time, it's a good idea to provide them with different storage options for stowing their belongings. In a winter house, where people often travel with a more comprehensive wardrobe of cold-weather gear, sportswear, and equipment, this is particularly necessary. And storage, in my opinion, should be just as stylish as the rest of your home. Beyond basic closets and built-ins, I chose antique pieces—luggage racks, wardrobes, dressers, cabinets, and the like—to complete the storage scenario. In this room, an antique pine armoire lined with the black-and-white toile used throughout the room tidily keeps guests' things tucked behind doors with chicken wire. Elaborate key tassels in the door locks add a finishing touch as well as a bit of color. In my search for supplementary storage, I also like to look for pieces that amuse or inspire conversation rather than "match" the rest of the room. Oddly, it's just that offbeat note that makes a space feel right. Case in point: placed between the beds in this room, a quirky turquoise chest of drawers (presumably once used by a chemist—I hope!) has labels for "cocaine," "opium," "cyanide," "arsenic," etc. I chose it because it made me laugh and fit within its allotted space! It is also functional, and holds a lamp made out of an antique Chinese tea canister and a phone hidden away in one drawer for aesthetic reasons and to make room for bedside necessities. (I have yet to encounter an attractive telephone—a design opportunity for someone, no?)

The comfort of my guests always guides the room's design. Good light and a comfortable chair for reading, and a quiet place to write and have a light snack are all important considerations.

LITTLE LUXURIES

GUEST HOSPITALITY AND AMENITIES

No matter how beautifully a guest room is decorated, it must be inviting, comfortable, and well stocked. You can make your guests feel truly at home by stocking their rooms with the things they might need—and then some. I recommend going the extra mile to really spoil your visitors. Before guests arrive, I decide who will occupy each room and choose special things I know each guest will enjoy. Preparations like these take very little time but add greatly to the ease and comfort of all who visit. It's always a luxury not to have to bother your host for what you need!

the basics and beyond A carafe of water (and, space permitting, a teapot), fresh flowers, clean towels, and a beautifully made bed are the basics. If you have room, store extra pillows, blankets, and throws in the closet. Padded hangers and a luggage stand are always appreciated. I will usually select some books from my library and new magazines based on guests' hobbies or interests; other special treats include chocolate or fruit I know they enjoy, a scented candle, and lavender sachets in closets and drawers.

winter extras Your guests will thank you for these winter necessities: extra-strength lip balm and body lotion, a hot-water bottle, a hair dryer, a variety of soaps and bath salts, special toiletries, and a warm robe or two.

THE BLUE-AND-YELLOW ROOM

Oddly shaped rooms present both a decorating challenge and an opportunity. Add limited window exposures and poor natural light and you've got your decorating work cut out for you. Located on the house's lower level, this room had all of these issues and then some when we first bought the house. Ducts crossed part of the ceiling and the fireplace (recently installed, and at an angle to boot) came across as a hurried afterthought. What to do? My first instinct was to treat it like a hideaway. Because the room was below the stairs, it had that "secret" feeling, like an attic room tucked under the eaves. In fact, I'm usually drawn to these types of spaces. When I was a child, I was always squirreling myself away in a corner of my grandmother's attic and rifling through old trunks. Sometimes, I would make my way high up in the old spruce trees. These were my personal spaces where no one could find me, and I was free to hang out and daydream. I decided to try to capture that same feeling of escape and coziness in this room.

The room had only one window, so I knew I had to stick with a lighter palette for the best results. The soft blues, ivories, and white of the wallpaper, tiles, carpet, and quilt give the space a restful unity, while a buttery yellow Pierre Frey fabric on the bed and curtains helps to compensate for the limited light. The colors are quiet, the contrast low, and the mood soothing. When designing homes for my husband and myself, I always find there is another room beyond our own where I could retreat just as comfortably. For me, this guest room would be my "second home" in this house.

The bed needed to be special, but anything with a canopy or too much going on overhead might have made the room feel cramped. I found the antique corona placed over the bed in England. It was the perfect embodiment of the statement I wanted to make in the context of this room—not too much, but just

I encourage creating decorative possibilities. Here, an antique butter press with a wheat pattern has been stained and refashioned to hold back bedside curtains.

quiet and soothing

A CENTURY OF

enough. The yellow bed hangings are lined with a delicate blue-and-white geometric pattern. The hangings lend the room a softness and height, and echo the shape and trim of the curtains on the window at the other side of the room.

One true selling point of this room is its fireplace—none of the other guest bedrooms (save the guest apartment) can lay claim to this same benefit. When we bought the house, this fireplace had been built into the wall at an angle diagonal to the bed. The surrounding wall was left blank, and I felt the opening needed framing. The idea was to call attention to the fireplace. I lined the wall with blue-and-white delft tiles, which gave the fireplace greater character. The dark-stained mantelpiece and crown molding were added to punctuate the room with a darker tone, which is echoed in the carved French garden mirror above the fire. Flanking the mirror are two reverse-glass paintings depicting Dutch ladies in a nod to the heritage of the tiles and a pair of tole floral cachepots for balance and symmetry.

To the right of the fireplace sits a provincial Italian desk, painted in a soft aqua. It features an arrangement of books and accessories, as well as a constantly rotating assortment of artwork and decorative objects that may reappear in many different places over time. These changes keep the rooms feeling fresh and let us all enjoy a variety of favorite treasures. The rush-bottomed wood desk chair adds still more texture to a room already filled with it. On top of the desk, a miniature chair was upholstered in keeping with the room's scheme. It sometimes rests on a stack of books that act as a pedestal.

Guests who sleep in this room enjoy one of my favorite bathrooms in the house. The walls are lined with blue-and-white Portuguese tiles and warmed with antique chestnut cabinets. The heated limestone floor is a special luxury on a cold winter morning.

I love the decorative and functional merits of tiles. In this room, delft tiles are used to frame the opening of the fireplace, while in the adjoining bath Portuguese tiles create the backsplash for the sink.

THE GUEST APARTMENT

Much of the lower level of the Aspen house was originally designated for a caretaker's living space, but I redesigned it as a guest apartment so that families and others coming for a longer stay could relax in a mini ski lodge of their own. Entirely self-contained, the apartment has its own separate entrance and its own kitchen and dining area as well as a living room, bedroom, and bath. Visitors staying here can make themselves a light meal or snack, settle with the kids in front of the fire with games or a movie, or just enjoy some quiet, private time away from the rest of the household. It was an extra treat to design this complete space—almost as if I got to design two houses in one! The French-country style of the apartment is slightly more casual than the upstairs, but there are similar textures and palettes that help tie it in with the rest of the house. And unlike the other guest rooms, where the style was driven by the beds, the apartment allowed me to experiment with concepts for guests' common rooms. Many of the same decorating and space planning ideas described here could be applied to almost any apartment, small home, or guest room.

The spacious and open main room serves as both the living and the dining areas. In such spaces, large pieces of furniture can be deployed to help create a sense of place. For example, the Knole-style sofa and a desk are situated back-to-back to visually divide the room while maintaining the general openness. The sofa has a back and arms of equal height, which creates a

The sofa and desk are situated

back-to-back to **visually** divide the room.

For your guests' enjoyment, thoughtful gestures might include stocking the desk with writing paper and nice pens, or placing a lovely magnifying glass near a stack of books for ease in reading.

CAFE
DU
LOIRET

room-within-a-room feeling not unlike some of the beds in the other guest bedrooms. Similarly, the effect is cozy, warm, and enveloping. The desk placed immediately behind it offers all-important writing and work space and also provides a light for anyone reading on the sofa. I've equipped the desk with a cup of pens and pencils, fresh flowers, and, of course, books. There is also a magnifying glass—I usually end up putting one on every desk I have. Not only are they useful, but the antique versions are often quite beautiful. The one here, with its handle made from a twisted branch, seemed made for a winter house. Adding themed accessories like this one is a simple way to temporarily transform any house into a winter house.

The desk faces the dining area, which is defined by an extra-high-backed banquette that creates a strong architectural statement and anchors the corner of the room. It's an intimate nook, and the tufted upholstery and mix of suede and needlepoint pillows add both warmth and comfort. A nickel-plated light fixture and vintage café sign above and the zinc-wrapped table all evoke the casual spirit of a bistro. It's a place where I hope guests like to linger, eating and talking or reading the newspaper. Like the main dining table of the house, this table is also often dressed with a pair of candlesticks or globe hurricanes and a rustic floral arrangement.

I love the rich patina and highly textured grain of old wood and have used it where I can throughout the house. The guest apartment is no exception—the rich caramel color of antique French chestnut is everywhere. In the dining area, a counter made of this wood provides a convenient perch for a quick meal or a place for a guest to sit while keeping the cook company. Beyond the counter, shelves in the same chestnut hold tole trays and creamware, faience, and pewter dishes and serving pieces. The heftier

H

HOMEWORK

LAMP SHADES

Ah, the poor neglected lamp shade. Often overlooked, it is actually a critical design component and just as important as the lamp it sits atop. In the same way a bad hair day can ruin your whole ensemble, a bad lamp shade can make your whole room look off. Thankfully, it's a relatively easy problem to fix if you remember a few essential shade factors.

shape Consider the style of the lamp and its context within the style of your room. What is the shape of the base? Will the lamp reside in a narrow space? How far will it sit from the wall?

proportion Your eye will tell you what's right—when in doubt, carry the lamp base along to your local shade shop and let the experts guide you.

style This is a matter of personal preference, with appropriateness as your guiding principle (unless there is a print involved; see "Color and Pattern"); choose from gathered, stretched, knife pleat, box pleat, cuffed.

color and pattern Depending on the look you wish to achieve, you should choose to cover your shade with a color or a pattern that is compatible with the rest of your room. For example, a red lamp shade that echoes the red found in the floral pattern of an upholstered wall would add some richness and strong contrast to a reading lamp in a corner, while a matching toile shade in an all-toile room would simply blend in. Think about how the light will come through the shade. For example, a dark shade will not provide a lot of light and is best for places where ambient light is more important than reading light. A pattern may also impact the style of the shade: for a large-scale pattern, a stretched shade might be a better choice than a gathered one so that you can see the pattern; however, a mini print can stand up to gathering.

details Be mindful of balance when adding trim: some trimmed bottom edges require a small detail at the top to prevent the shade from becoming bottom heavy. *Never* use trims with a high sheen—choose those with a high natural fiber content or do without. You can always add trim later.

linings I prefer simple polyester linings because they last longer than silk. I usually choose an off-white lining with an off-white shade, but I sometimes opt for a very pale pink lining with a deep ivory shade. Dark red or green shades lined in pale yellow gold have a pretty glow. I think white looks too stark against dark colors.

the palette is a rich mix of clarets, browns, and golds

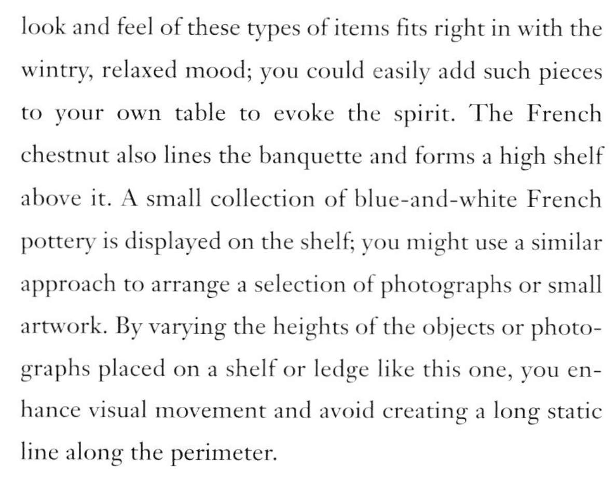

look and feel of these types of items fits right in with the wintry, relaxed mood; you could easily add such pieces to your own table to evoke the spirit. The French chestnut also lines the banquette and forms a high shelf above it. A small collection of blue-and-white French pottery is displayed on the shelf; you might use a similar approach to arrange a selection of photographs or small artwork. By varying the heights of the objects or photographs placed on a shelf or ledge like this one, you enhance visual movement and avoid creating a long static line along the perimeter.

At the opposite end of the room, a door separates the bedroom from the main living space. Inside, the palette is a rich mix of clarets, browns, and golds, and there is a wealth of textures. The bed, bedside tables, and an overhead arch with bookshelves and downlights are all built right into an alcove to maximize the limited space. Drawers underneath offer extra room for clothing storage and a place to stow bulky items like extra duvets. On the wall I used one of my favorite means of displaying art: vintage black-and-white photographs of Paris from an old portfolio were each framed individually in simple, matching frames then hung as a group. With lighting supplied from above and the phone hidden in a drawer, there is plenty of room on the small bedside tables for reading material, a water carafe, or whatever else one needs to relax comfortably. On the bed, guests will find a layered mix of patterns and the luxurious winter textures of an appliquéd velvet pillow and faux-fur blanket.

Layering of pattern and texture was an operating principle for this room, from the paisley throw on the windowpane-plaid chair (below) to the mélange of patterns that makes up the bed (opposite).

"I wake up expecting things."

Fleur Cowles

A SCHEME FOR

a Bedroom

1

2

3

Ideal for a winter-house bedroom or guest room, this scheme draws from a simplified palette of red, white, and black. With a mix of matelasse, classic checks and paisley, a window-pane pattern, and a bucolic scenic print with an alpine theme, there are a variety of things to draw from, and they all work together. But while this scheme is simple it is also versatile. You can choose your fabrics from a perspective of red and white with touches of black, or white and black with punches of red. The red floral (top left) would be lovely for curtains, while the paisley (center left) would work well on a sofa and could be complemented by pillows in just about any of the other fabrics. The faux fur (bottom right) is just for fun; it would make a cozy throw, an ottoman cover, or pillows.

4

5

6
7
8
9
10
11
12
13

Decoratin

g for Fun

“Always put something mad on top of something very good, or something very good on top of something mad.”

Geoffrey Bennison

3

Decorating for Fun

THE HOLIDAYS TRIMMING THE TREE THE TABLE

My apologies to the inimitable Dorothy Draper and her celebrated book of nearly the same name as this chapter. Isn't all decorating "fun"? Well, yes. Decorating the rooms of a winter house is fun in and of itself, but it ultimately serves the higher purpose of furnishing your home. I am always looking for more chances to decorate, and a winter house offers two opportunities for you to experiment and reinvent yourself that are purely for enjoyment: the holidays and the table.

Perhaps it goes without saying that holiday decorating is a major part of winter-house festivities. Most people get in the spirit and dress up their homes in some way, whether indoors or out, to create a jolly atmosphere. Cards and packages arriving in the mail always spread a little cheer. Spend a few afternoons carefully selecting paper and ribbons to graciously wrap presents, then celebrate family traditions around a beautifully trimmed Christmas tree.

In a winter house, there are as many occasions to set a pretty table as there are meals to be shared. Holidays like Thanksgiving, Christmas, and the New Year bring everyone together, and winter cocktail or dinner parties are scheduled with friends. For these events, I like to make each place setting special and interesting through my choices of tableware, accessories, and luscious flowers and greenery.

The Holidays

This time of year presents a chance to try something new—perhaps a wintry theme or color scheme—whether in moderation through small details and embellishments or as an all-embracing transformation in every room. A treasure trove of materials provides inspiration—fresh evergreen garlands, winter fruits, glittering ornaments, ribbons and wrappings. Even if a Christmas tree plays the starring role in your holiday decor, you can always extend your concepts or color palette to include your choice of gift wrappings as well. I like to experiment with new color combinations, and I don't hold back when it comes to outfitting our Aspen home with holiday finery. Having our house dressed inside and out adds to the joy and anticipation of the season.

During the holidays, anything is fair decorating game. A plate of personalized after-dinner cookies (above) might be inspired by the "stockings hung on the chimney with care," while a bare window or door frame (opposite) feels more festive with a wreath or a garland in place.

DECKING THE HALLS . . . AND BEYOND

For me, one of the most essential decorating elements to give a visual boost to the season is greenery, greenery, and more greenery! Many winter greens have a wonderful fragrance, and all add gorgeous natural textures to an environment. I described how I use greenery outdoors in chapter 1, but it's the idea of bringing the outside in that I find especially appealing. I like things a little on the wild and woodsy side, and I love creating an indoor forest with fresh garlands and branches. Arrangements of various evergreens in different containers perch on top of cabinets in the living room and in the kitchen, and garlands line the fireplace mantels and the banister and balcony of the stairs. A few spruce or pine cuttings tucked in among flowers are a pretty way to give tabletop arrangements a seasonal flair. As much as I love them, evergreens and firs aren't the only game in town. I'm also fond of mimosa, tendrils of Rothschild lilies, forced bulbs of amaryllis and narcissus, and beautiful green magnolia leaves with their suedelike brown undersides. Seasonal fruits such as pomegranates and lady apples can be used to fill an urn or a cachepot on a tabletop for a harvesttime look. I also like to incorporate fruits such as clementines, kumquats, and figs still on the branch. Other natural elements, like pheasant and other bird feathers, also add texture when mixed in with florals.

A quirky Alpine chair provides a woodsy, whimsical perch near the fireplace.

Tropical fruits and orchids provide in our otherwise indoor

the essential contrast
evergreen landscape.

LITTLE LUXURIES

FRAGRANCE

Fragrance is a great memory detonator; we all have associations that are awakened by a particular fragrance. There is something to be said for the power of a memorable scent. When you close your eyes and take a whiff of something delicious, your mind and body instantly relax. So naturally, I am a proponent of most things scented at our Aspen house. I am not advocating the kind of all-consuming fragrance that stops you dead in your tracks; I prefer more subtle infusions that delight the nose in such a way that you are hardly aware you are smelling anything at all. Lavender, fig, and winter greens like cypress are some of my favorites.

scented candles Easy to move and replace, scented candles are ideal anywhere but are particularly effective in the foyer, where you greet people, and in hallways and powder rooms.

sachets You can buy sachets or make your own: fill small silk drawstring bags with your favorite scent, bundle them in a vintage hankie, and tie with ribbon, or make a little slipcover from a bit of antique fabric. The best thing about sachets is how unobtrusive they are—put them in a clothes drawer, in a desk drawer, under a pillow, behind a radiator, or under a sofa cushion, or hang one from a doorknob or clothes hanger, and don't forget to tuck one inside a suitcase. You can even place a bowlful of sachets on a table to perfume the air.

other ideas Place a basket of fragrant and colorful flower petals mixed with lemon and orange peels in a living room, a bedroom, or a study; use scented linen spray for bedding in the master bedroom and guest rooms; stock all bathrooms with scented soaps, bath oils, and lotions.

"It's the flowers you choose, the music you play, the smile you have waiting."

AUDREY HEPBURN

During some holiday seasons, it seems as though every level space in the house has some sort of container bursting with flowers and greenery. I can't help it—for me, it's all about creating the feeling of an indoor forest!

Trimming the Tree

For those who celebrate Christmas, the most personal winter-house decoration of all is the Christmas tree, bedecked with special ornaments and trimmings. I can remember spending hours as a child stringing popcorn and fresh cranberries to make our annual garland; my tastes have changed since then, but I still treasure the memories. There are many approaches to decorating a Christmas tree—you can stick with a particular palette or theme for your ornaments and decorations or trim your tree with anything and everything you love in a quirky jumble. Whatever your preference, the tree is often a focal point and a gathering place for opening presents and other merry moments.

It's a common decorating premise that if you buy the things you love, inevitably they will find a home. The same could be said for the ornaments on your Christmas tree, whether they are given to you or you collect them over the years yourself!

With its double-height ceilings, our living room was made to play host to a skyscraping Christmas tree (although we usually end up having to remove a couple of pieces of furniture from the room to accommodate its girth!). Such a large tree is home to the many ornaments we've collected or been given, and over the years our tree has evolved into one with a palette of white, green, and silver. Some of the ornaments have a little twinkle, such as snowflakes made of crystal beads or balls covered with white or metallic fabric and ribbons and pearls. Others are miniature replicas of things we love or love to do—mine include scaled-down pieces of furniture and little garden benches and watering cans. Some ornaments are odes to winter fun, like the figures of skiers and skaters. To enhance the fragrance of the tree, I tie bunches of lavender with metallic ribbon and place them randomly throughout the boughs. Lavender's scent is delicious, and the purple color complements the ornaments' palette. I'm also a big fan of stopping in at holiday craft fairs and Junior League events to shop for handcrafted ornaments; there's always someone selling incredible handmade treasures. But my favorites are the ornaments my mother made for me—they are reminders of her presence during the holidays.

JOY

"There are definite advantages to making something big out of a lot of little things."

CHUCK CLOSE

The house's prevailing influence of garden and nature is evident even on the Christmas tree. Shimmering oak leaves, maple leaves, and a jeweled dragonfly find a home.

some ornaments
are odes to

winter fun

With its antler and moose motifs, plaids, and deep palette, this manly scheme would be appropriate for a billiard room, a study, a library, or a boy's room. The rich colors and patterns create layers with depth. The paisley with looped fringe trim (top right) would be great for a pillow detail. The plaid (bottom left) would be a sophisticated choice for a chair, while the French check (bottom right) is a classic choice for the chair back. Just for fun, add a sofa or club chair in corduroy; heavy, blanket-like curtains could be made to complement the scheme, perhaps in a paisley.

5

6

7

A SCHEME FOR

a Gentleman's Room

8

9

10

11

12

13

One season, my gift wrap was inspired by the outdoors. Each gift was topped with something reusable—velvet leaves and flowers, speckled feathers, or snowflakes in crystal, wood and silver.

GIFTS AND WRAPPINGS

When my mother was still living, my extended family would hold big Christmas celebrations at my grandmother's house. With my aunt and all my uncles and their children (always a growing number!), we decided to have a Secret Santa–style exchange. It was always great fun and we *tried* not to reveal whose name we drew. Now we open our presents on Christmas Eve after dinner and dessert, and we save one present to open at breakfast the next morning. We take turns, and everyone squirms as we tear into the paper.

Every holiday season I have loads of presents to prepare, both personally for family and friends and professionally for my staff and the many people I work with on projects. I do a lot of shopping as part of my work, and I buy gifts as I see them throughout the year. To keep track of gifts, I started a present journal arranged by recipient so I have a record of what I've bought and given to everyone on my list; in this journal I also record presents I've received and the date I sent a thank-you note. The journal is a handy way to stay organized, and it is a memento of the generosity of so many people.

With this many presents passing through my house, the evenings of nearly two solid weeks before Christmas are dedicated to getting everything wrapped! Having done this for a number of years, I've discovered the most efficient and aesthetically pleasing way to address this mountain of gifts is to create a signature look for the season and wrap all the gifts that way. Sometimes clients ask me to create a wrapping program for them. You can certainly do this for yourself: start with something that inspires you—a ribbon in a particular color, a bag of beaded snowflakes, a few velvet leaves—and take things from there. In the past I've been inspired by everything from a swatch of red toile to a very pale peach amaryllis bloom. Two of my favorite palettes have included a woodsy theme of green and brown with chartreuse accents and a softer, elegant palette of white, green, and silvery sage accented with touches of lavender.

I also like to think "outside the box," so to speak, and consider alternatives to conventional wrapping paper. One idea is to use wallpaper; it is sturdy and available in sophisticated colors and patterns that don't necessarily scream Christmas. I like papers in classic stripes and patterns as well as those that

mimic my favorite textures, like shagreen or faux bois. If you find a pattern you like, order a roll or two. I take a "leftovers" approach and use my remnants from decorating or buy discontinued patterns. Your local decorating supply center may be willing to part with sample books slated for disposal, and closeout sales at home stores often feature rolls at a bargain. Making your own papers, with the help of a photocopier, is a personalized concept. I have copied an assemblage of images from a winter-themed inspiration board I have and also enlarged some of the designs from a portfolio of bookbinding endpapers I bought in a Paris flea market to use as wrapping paper. Old letters with elegant handwriting can also be copied. Antique books written in foreign languages and printed on luxurious paper, old documents, and pieces of sheet music can make a graphic statement. For truly special gifts, I have taken actual pages from these books to use as wrappings; part of the fun for the recipient is trying to guess what the words say. (Of course, you can use these methods to design beautifully wrapped gifts at any time of the year.)

Gift tags, bows, and decorative ornaments are integral finishing touches: take a few creative liberties and assemble your own. Recycle the faces of old holiday or winter-themed greeting cards and adhere them to pieces of colored paper, ink-stamp a plain manila tag with your monogram, or photocopy a small picture of your family. These tags are an extension of the gift within and can be used in other ways long after a gift has been opened and enjoyed. For example, a bundle of cinnamon sticks can be tossed on a fire for fragrance or used to flavor drinks. Pin a silk flower to a sweater, tuck a feather in a hat. Little trinkets, such as an oak leaf charm or a bunch of millinery or craft fruits, find a second life as Christmas ornaments.

Organization is the key to everything—your clothes, your books, your . . . whatever. You may covet a whole room where your wrapping supplies are artfully arrayed but it's not often a reality. So wherever you keep your paper rolls, ribbons, scissors, and tape—in a corner of your home office, in a closet, or in a drawer—it's important to organize your tools. That way, when you're ready to get down to business in your own version of Santa's workshop, you'll know what you have and it will be ready to use.

A trip to New York's flower district always proves fruitful when I'm looking for items to decorate my gifts. Many craft-supply stores and notions departments also offer creative decorations for wrapping.

"The manner of giving is worth more than the gift."

Pierre Corneille

The principles for using patterns when decorating your home can also be applied to your gift wrap. Mix-and-match pairings, tonal combinations, or dramatic contrasts easily move from a room to the wrap.

The Table

As decorating elements go, the table is a vital one; it is the singular piece of furniture that draws people together face-to-face to share not just food but conversation. The table is the heart of having a good time. One of the great pleasures of entertaining is the opportunity to create new combinations for the table. Thanks to the various events that occur in a winter house—pre-ski breakfasts, weekend brunches, lively dinners and cocktail parties, holiday feasts, and other celebrations—you can play with the look of your table each time you set it. I want to pick everything, experiment, and keep playing with it all until it feels right. I believe that even informal meals should be treated as memorable occasions, and I take pleasure in setting the table every time, whether for a casual breakfast or for a formal dinner. You can develop a scheme for your table through your choice of china, linens, accessories, and flowers.

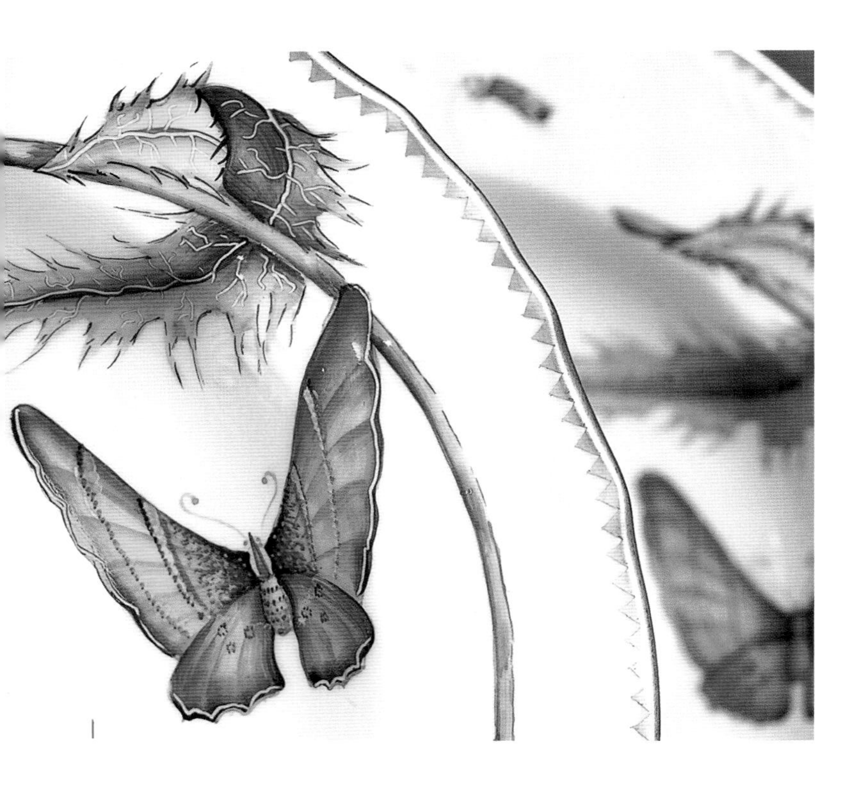

New hand-painted china from Anna Weatherley (above) is combined in the cupboard with English teapots, French faience, and Wedgwood creamware.

AN ECLECTIC COLLECTION

Table settings for a winter house are no different than any others when it comes to the basics. If you host large groups of guests or have a big family, you may need a few things to assist in feeding a crowd, like generous serving platters, large bowls, and tureens. But what makes your table feel special is your choice of textures, colors, and embellishments—not to mention your enthusiasm! The pleasing effect flows from the combination, not from any single object. That being said, I can never seem to stop adding to my eclectic hoard of tableware. In my travels and on shopping trips, I always keep an eye out for interesting new and antique items for the table. Each piece of china, set of linens, or decoration is a memento of the experience as well as a part of some future table setting.

I inherited the tableware gene from my grandmother, who worked in the china department of Miller & Rhoads department store in Richmond, Virginia, for more than twenty years. Admittedly, I've overindulged this addiction on many occasions and therefore need lots of room to keep everything organized and accessible. Our Aspen house has no centrally located storage area like a butler's pantry, so I keep my tableware in five different places.

the pleasing effect flows from

the combination

A pine cabinet in the living room holds some of the more unusual and decorative serving pieces: a faux cabbage tureen, a faience tureen, and Victorian silver-plate meat platters. The large dual cabinet that separates the kitchen and dining area contains glass and china, all organized by type and use on the shelves. One cabinet houses good barware, wineglasses, everyday glassware, and water carafes, plus some salt cellars and a few decorative items. My cache of good bone china is in the other cabinet—sets as well as my "4s, 6s, and 8s," a collection of random dishes in said denominations whose purchases I rationalized by telling myself "they'll go with anything." Everyday china and luncheon plates are kept in the kitchen cabinets.

Another storage spot is a hideaway pantry closet that we created in the space under the stairs leading to the lower level of the house. Inside is years of accumulations from my shopping excursions: chargers in wood, silver plate, pewter, and cane; flatware with handles of horn and rosewood, as well as serving utensils and carving knives with horn or antler handles; overscale nineteenth-century spoons made of coin silver for hearty soups and stews; an assortment of heavy crystal goblets; plus tea sets and odd teapots that guests can take on a tray to their rooms. I also store unique place-card holders plus assorted antiques and other decorations here. Last but not least is my collection of linens, which is housed in two big cabinets in the mudroom, to the right and left of the sink.

Carving sets, serving pieces, flatware, and cups in horn are stored in a cupboard built specifically for this purpose. A large antique cabbage leaf ceramic tureen is used for serving soups for a dinner buffet.

For me, part of composing a great table setting is having a variety of pieces to choose from to fit the mood and occasion. Themes build naturally, and you don't necessarily have to go out and look for objects to fit within them—these things tend to find us.

WINTER CHINA

Beautiful china instantly sets the tone and the mood. I rotate a couple of different china patterns, many of which have a woodland or botanical design. Some of my favorite pieces are decorated with faux bois, a simulated woodgrain styling, which looks right at home on the table in Aspen. One set of American plates is impressed with a faux-bois texture in the clay and a golden brown glaze. Another set of plates I had made in Paris at David Hicks has a faux-bois pattern on the border and my monogram painted on the inside. The monogram was taken from an eighteenth-century book of monograms by the court cartographer of Louis XIV, Mavelot. I mix these plates with antique French dishes decorated with leaves, nuts, and wintry-looking plants in autumnal tones of brown, orange, chestnut, and taupe. I sometimes mix in selections from a beautiful series of plates hand-painted with leaves and thistles in a palette of ocher, violet, and tobacco that works perfectly with our house. Mixing china patterns and tableware sometimes takes courage, but once you've done it, you realize how many new possibilities you may already have in your cupboards. And, as a result of combining, you immediately increase the number of settings you can create.

If you don't have the resources or the storage space to accommodate a varied assortment of china, you can always use whatever you have and give your table a winter flavor through your choice of accessories and special items. Serving pieces made of wood or horn and a platter or a tea set in a wintry palette or pattern are good choices. Our coffee service of Paris porcelain has a painted motif that is in tune with much of the artwork in the house. On each demitasse cup and on the coffeepot, a man is enjoying himself playing sports, hunting, or fishing. To carry on the woodsy spirit, I sometimes set out glass salt cellars that look like a nut cracked in half or ceramic vases that look like mini white logs. Plain white china can evoke a wintry mood with unique pieces like these. Place them all on a dark-colored tablecloth of spruce, garnet red, or deep blue for an elegant and dramatic contrast.

Variations on a theme—part of the enjoyment of entertaining comes with the experimenting you do in between events.

Jim
Bonnie

TABLE LINENS

The real treasures of my table are my collection of linens. My appreciation for these table essentials was handed down to me from my grandmother, whose Sunday afternoon buffets were a family tradition. Even as a child, I was awed by the ease with which she entertained our large family and the beauty of the linens she used to set the table. I loved the variety of the fabrics, with clean variations on white and their details of lace and embroidery. I still own some of the linens my grandmother embroidered, and cherish the memories they evoke.

My favorite table linens are a mix of the old and new, the elegant and offbeat, and crisp white and vivid colors. Wherever I go, I always keep an eye out for table linens to buy. Some are purchased as gifts for friends or clients, and others are for my own tables. Finding pretty cloths or napkins with monograms that match my initials or those of friends is always a bonus, and it does happen. When it doesn't, I buy the antiques and then have them monogrammed. My linen collection includes many different styles, from embroidered to Indian-patterned prints to linens made from unexpected fabrics. Many feature some kind of small, special detail such as a scalloped edging or a delicate motif. For formal meals I'll lay out an antique linen tablecloth or layer a colored cloth underneath an incredible crocheted tablecloth. As I recombine linens for each new table setting, I like to think that some I've chosen might become a legacy for my family, just as my grandmother's linens are for me.

Linens are a great way to both personalize and winterize your table, since they let you try on colors and effects without making as much of a costly commitment as china or flatware. The key is to have fun and go with your table-setting instincts. And remember, your tables should always entertain you as well as your guests!

"A good soup promises a great meal."

Fleur Cowles

EVERYTHING IN ITS PLACE

Setting a beautiful table starts with organization. How your china, flatware, serving accessories, and linens are stored is crucial to the success of any table; you can't get inspired if you can't see what you have to work with! In addition, if you have invested in quality objects for your home, it only makes sense to protect them so you can enjoy them for a long time. In my house, napkins, place mats, and tablecloths are laid out on shelves; drawers or even stacking boxes can serve the same purpose. When linens are stored so that you can see them together, your eyes can visually mix and match them in fresh and interesting ways. I prefer storing linens flat. Thin boards covered with quilted linen are inserted as dividers in between each set so it's easy to pick up an entire grouping and move it around without wrinkling. Objects like place-card holders or special table objects are stored topically in drawers or boxes. My large silver pieces are wrapped in protective tarnish-resistant cloths, and flatware is placed in drawers lined with the same.

If your own storage space does not permit you to have everything in plain view and your table items are stored in an attic or elsewhere, you may wish to create a tableware and accessories workbook of sorts. This is a useful idea even if you do have ample and accessible storage space. Photograph the different pieces you have and arrange them by category in a photo album, notebook, or journal. When it comes time to set your table, you can flip through your book to remind yourself of what you have. You may even wish to capture favorite table settings on film and add the photographs to the workbook for ease in re-creating the settings later. I also keep scrapbooks to record entertaining in our Aspen house. Menus, guest lists, place cards, invitations, and pictures of flower arrangements are all there, creating a full record of each party that I can look back on for purposes practical or sentimental. Scrapbooks like these become a record of your life, so make the most of them!

In my collection of tableware and linens, motifs of flowers and greenery are represented in so many ways—printed, embroidered, even woven right into the fabric.

SETTING THE SCENE

In preparation for setting the table, I often think about the menu and work backward to choose which dishes will best complement what will be served, and from there I move on to choosing the linens. I find that an organized approach, which might include a "dry run" setup the day or evening before, helps reduce any predinner stress.

I'm a firm believer in using beloved pieces every day. I use my silver at every meal. For informal meals I tend to choose from the blue-edged creamware or other ceramic patterns, while for formal meals I'll use the bone china. I like using odd sets of plates in combination, sometimes up to three patterns at once. I also like to cluster glass and silver pieces in combinations of old or new, and, of course, I like to mix and match them, too. Deciding on the flowers is an important aspect of any table I set. I might choose to decorate every place with mini Christmas trees or individual flower arrangements in unexpected containers. Or I'll choose to create one long floral landscape running the length of the table.

My goal is to design an environment where everyone feels as if he or she is at his or her own private table; each place setting is its own universe, a table within a table. One simple way to accomplish this (as well as indicate where you'd like everyone to sit) is to use place cards. Tented cards are the simplest approach, but depending on the overall look of the table I like to use plain, flat cards with decorative holders such as little silver acorns and leaves, silver pheasants, or antique vermeil game animals. For some special meals, I might also put a little favor along with the place card, such as a lavender sachet in a silk or linen drawstring bag. We keep the place cards on the table until the first course is finished; then they are removed with the dishes. That way, everyone has a little time to learn the names of his or her neighbors!

A good table is one where everyone laughs and lingers till the bitter end, and it is always important for me when reviewing a guest list to figure out who's compatible, who doesn't know whom, who already sat next to whom at a previous party, and so on. In our house, I try to really mix things up to bring together people who might enjoy one another's company. And, to make sure we spend some time talking with all of our guests, my husband and I might swap places mid-dinner.

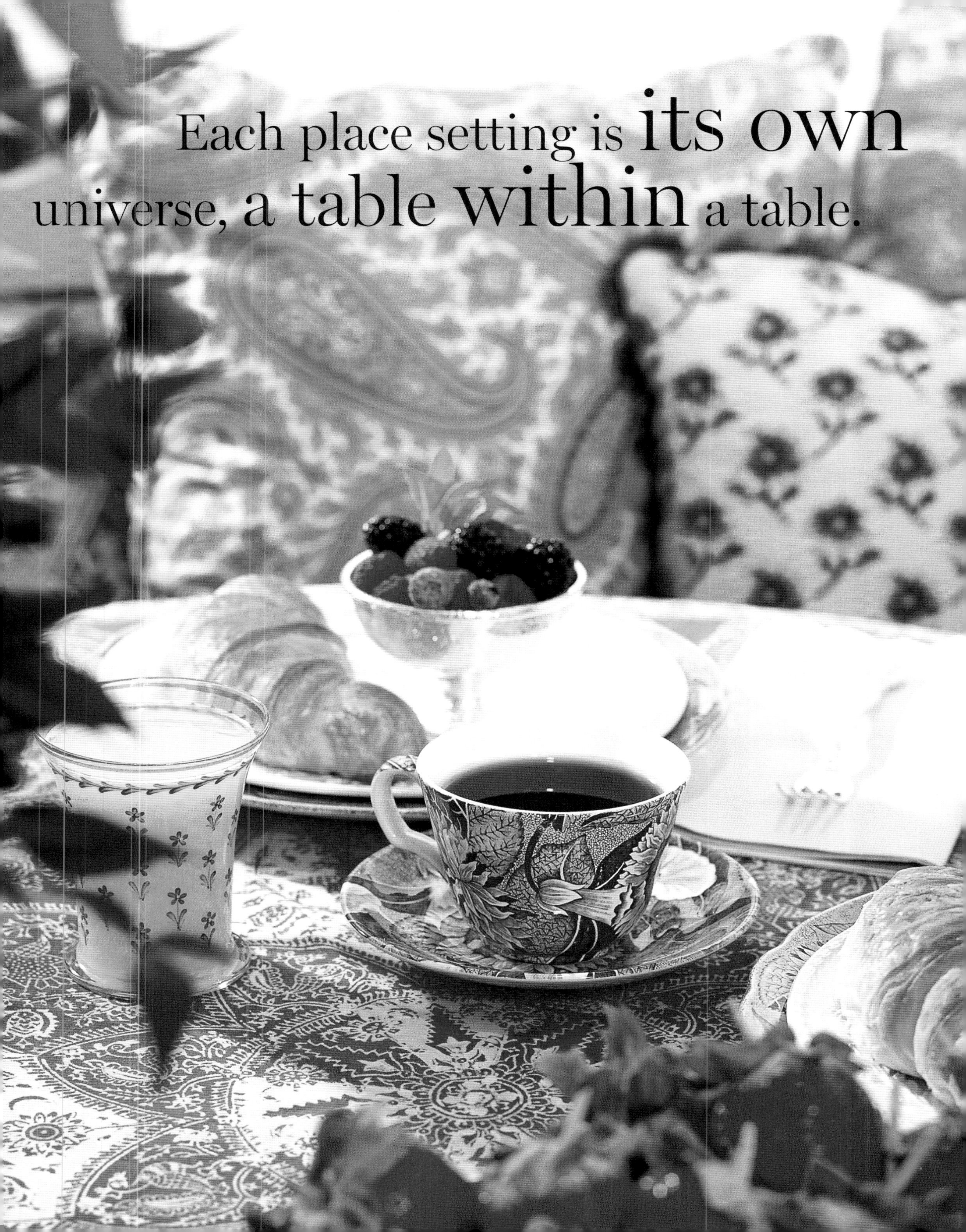

Each place setting is its own universe, a table within a table.

LITTLE LUXURIES

PLACE CARDS

When guests sidle up to a table before a meal and see a little placard marking their place with their name, they can't help but feel special. Family and friends alike will appreciate the thought you put into their seating. You'll also have some control over the social success of your event as you know your guests best. Place cards and their holders are one of the many elements on the table that help to set the scene. I always use some type, either simple cards or a combination of holders and cards.

papers and cards Tented cards are widely available in colors or with motifs to coordinate with your table setting. You can also choose to personalize them yourself. For one girls' weekend I hosted, my friend Anne Harris painted watercolors of flowers on each place card. Anne made this simple touch look effortless—just a brushstroke and voilà: a snowdrop or a violet. When I use place-card holders, I choose less-decorated cards, maybe a simple embossed sunflower, a pheasant, or an orange tree. Either way, I like to write a guest's name on both sides of the card so the guest can find his or her seat, and those sitting opposite can see the guest's name. Always write guests' names by hand with a nice pen: printed names on place cards are not very personal to me; in fact, it makes me feel as if I'm attending a convention!

place-card holders Many types of place-card holders are available, from a simple silver ball to more elaborate three-dimensional designs to suit a theme or a decor. I have collected a couple of different antique sets in shapes that echo the wintry, woodland table settings I like to create, with silver acorns and oak leaves and game animals among them. Miniature picture frames are also popular place-card holders and can be given to guests as a party favor.

alternatives In lieu of a traditional holder, you can attach place cards to something seasonal, such as a piece of fruit like a Seckel pear or a lady apple, or tie them to pairs of cherries still on the stem, or tuck them in the leaves of split artichokes. Unexpected objects that fit within a theme, such as copper plant markers for a garden-party luncheon, are also whimsical alternatives.

"He sees the debris of the table as still life."

Marcel Proust on Chardin

Enjoying

Yourself

"I cannot remember a time when I was not in love with them—with the books themselves, cover and binding and the paper they were printed on, with their weight and with their possession in my arms, captured and carried off to myself."

EUDORA WELTY

Enjoying Yourself

STAYING INSIDE HEADING OUTDOORS

In a winter house, you can sense the merriment in the air. Time spent in such a house excites all the senses—there's the comfort of luxurious wraps by the fire and down-filled duvets on the beds, the twinkle of candles and treasured objects that catch the eye, wonderful things to eat and drink set on a gorgeous table, the fragrance of fresh-cut evergreens and pots of paperwhite narcissus, and laughter and conversation floating through the rooms.

Of course, everyone has his or her own interpretation of "enjoying yourself." It's purely up to you to decide: Do I wish to be indoors or out? Do I want to spend time with a group of family and friends or be alone? Wherever your winter house is, and however you choose to create its atmosphere, when all is said and done the point is to relax and have a good time.

When I'm indoors at our house and have some time by myself, I like to catch up on favorite hobbies such as scrapbooking, journal writing, needlepoint, and reading—all things I don't often have enough free time to enjoy when I'm back in the bustle of New York City. For outdoor time, downhill skiing is our activity of choice. It's the perfect way to spend a fun-filled day with our houseguests. Wherever your winter house is, and however you choose to create its atmosphere, when all is said and done the point is to relax and have a good time.

Staying Inside

As the snow falls outside, there's a buzz indoors. Maybe everyone is taking a break from outdoor activities to rest weary bodies or it's just too cold out to venture much beyond the fireside. A group might gather for a friendly challenge—a board game, billiards, or whatever it is that gets your family laughing together. Or maybe it's time for a personal break, to relax and take refuge with a more solitary pursuit or hobby. Either way, there's plenty to do in a winter house.

A little friendly rivalry never hurt anyone—time indoors in a winter house is well spent over a classic board game in front of the fire.

GATHERING A GROUP

The cast of characters in a winter house is ever changing, making for a different good time each time you play host to a group of adults gathered for a ski weekend, a mix of family and friends for a celebration, or the young, old, and in between for the holidays. With so many individuals, it helps to have some sort of plan or activity where all can join in and enjoy one another's company.

Whenever we have family or friends staying with us in Aspen, we let everyone know the general schedule of meals and when most people will be going out on the mountain so they can plan other things they'd like to do as well as some personal time. But then there are more spontaneous moments, when everyone comes together to hang out. Often we play games; games are such "people gatherers" and intellectual exercise for those who have been pushing their bodies over moguls all day. We have boards enticingly set up for an easy game of chess, checkers, or backgammon. My own favorite is Scrabble, which always brings out a family's competitive side! What could be better than a blazing fire . . . a hot toddy . . . and a triple-word score?

Those type A folks who seek to continue the rowdy competition from the slopes can cue up in the billiard room. I always laugh at how a pool table really pulls people together, hooting and hollering as they neatly send a ball into the corner pocket. A workout room when we bought the house, this space on the lower level has been redesigned as a place where everyone, particularly the men, can gather before or after dinner or during cocktails.

dictionary
ROGET'S II

A SCHEME FOR a Family Room

7

9

8

What is it about the combination of blue and white that makes it a universal favorite? The fabrics and textures here could be adapted to any number of rooms.

Imagine walls covered in a blue-and-cream twill or a wallpaper of linen and grass cloth. Picture a pair of hearty benches in horsehair and sofas and club chairs in corduroy. A wing chair in a blue-green wool plaid and pillows in toiles or boucles, an oversized ottoman in a tapestry weave. In a corner of the room is a leather-topped game table with chairs covered in linen gingham. This is only one concept; now it's your turn.

12

10

11

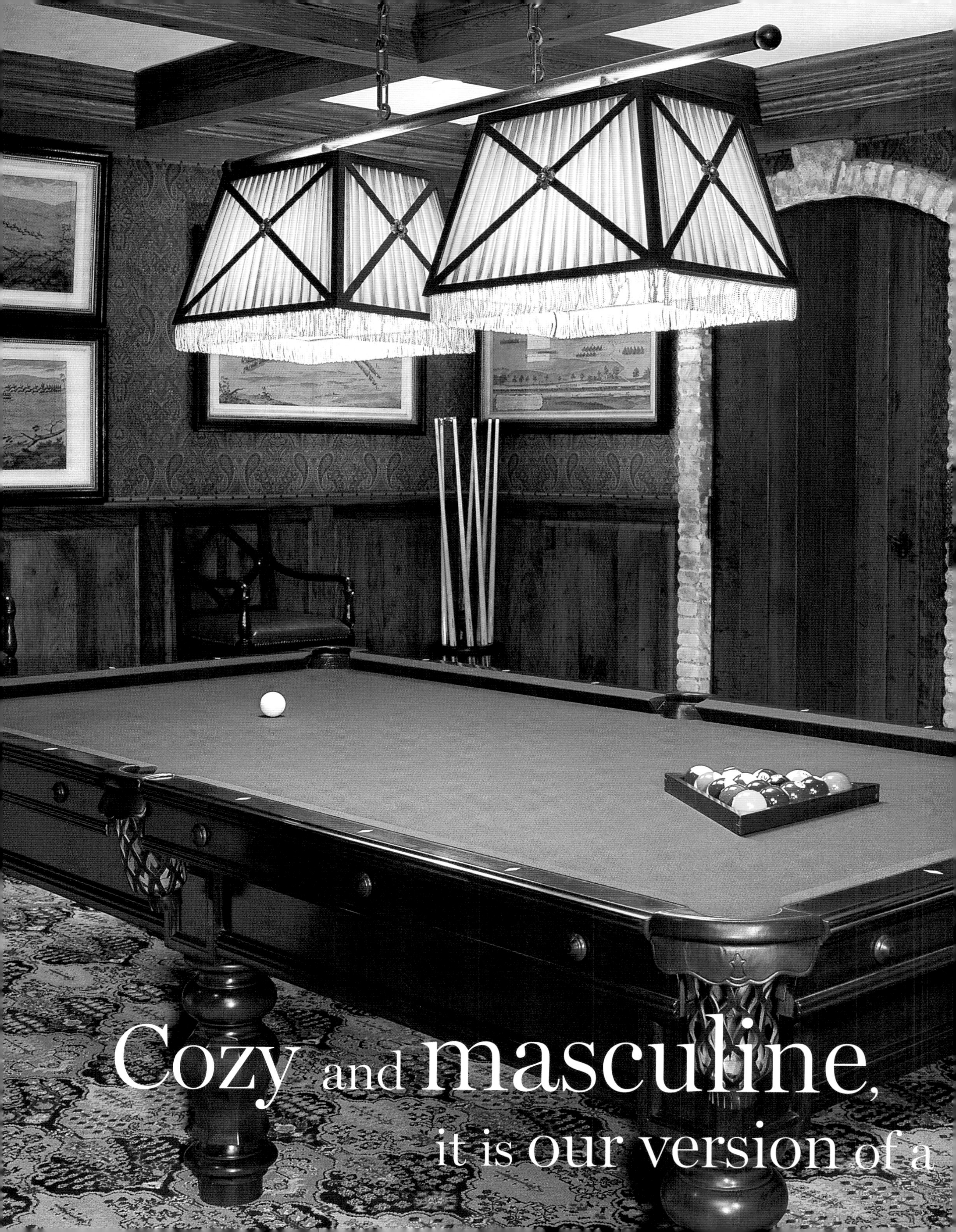

Cozy and masculine,
it is our version of a

Saturated with pattern, color, and texture, the room is cozy, yet masculine. The green paisley fabric, paneled antique chestnut on the walls, deep colors, nail-head trim, and framed engravings of military battle scenes create our version of a gentleman's club. The English-style billiard table sits in the center of the space with plenty of room for movement around it. Cues are stored on a rack in the corner. A pair of billiard chairs offers seating for a cheering section or those awaiting their turn at the table. An arched wooden door with a stone surround leads to the wine cellar. In the lock of the cellar door is an old key I found in a market in London; marked "Dormitory," it's a funny commentary on our Aspen house and its changing array of guests!

We were fortunate to inherit a wine cellar when we bought the house. My husband is a passionate wine aficionado, so this naturally became his own special domain—a retreat in which he can relax and enjoy a favorite pastime. He catalogs, records, and tags wines here. Tags help identify bottles without disturbing them and also note when a particular vintage is ready to drink. This is my husband's responsibility, and his pleasure. A table in the cellar serves as a wonderfully atmospheric spot for small winter gatherings like a wine tasting or an after-dinner sampling of wine and cheese. A big bowl filled with corks is a testament to the many bottles enjoyed here, and the eclectic mix of serving accessories in horn, oak, pewter, and crystal is typical of the combinations throughout the house. The labels from the bottles are pasted in my entertaining journals (I guess I record just about everything!); they can be reminders of a great wine, a great vintage, or just a great evening. Of course, you really don't need a separate room to enjoy wine; you can host tastings in your dining room or on a terrace, or in any other favorite, cozy spot.

H

HOMEWORK

FINISHING TOUCHES AND TRIMS

In the same way that a fantastic pair of earrings or a cuff bracelet finishes an outfit, special touches and trims add a certain je ne sais quoi to a room or a piece of furniture. These embellishments offer an opportunity to make a space personal.

beads Thousands of styles of beads exist to complement any room. Crystal beads sewn along the edge of a curtain provide a little icy twinkle. Beads along the edge of a pillow or a lamp shade are also pretty, and you can attach them to the ends of tiebacks. Just one word of caution: use restraint; you don't want to overdecorate with beads.

passementerie This category offers a wide selection of trims such as silk cords, braids, gimps, fringe, and frog closures. Cords and braids are especially versatile; apply them to nearly anything requiring an outlining type of detail: pillows, curtains, the edge of upholstered furniture. Special flourishes like knots and frog closures are beautiful when sewn to the corners of pillows or used on chair covers.

ribbon The question is not where you can use ribbon but where you *can't*! I enjoy finding places to use the antique ribbons I pick up on my travels, but there are also many new styles with old-world appeal, such as a ribbon I purchased that looks like petit point. I often apply a banded ribbon to a curtain edge and set it in a half inch or so from the edge as an alternative to traditional trim. Of course, you can dress all the usual suspects—pillows, lamp shades, hand towels, place mats, and napkins—with a bit of ribbon. Accent plain upholstery with sturdy ribbons: I incorporated an antique needlepoint bellpull into the center of the velvet used to cover a slipper chair, but I could just as easily have used a tapestry ribbon.

tape and nail head I often finish off an upholstered wall with nail-head trim on tape. The trim doesn't actually apply the fabric to the wall but adds an extra layer of decorative detail and provides a clean, finished edge. Try a similar application on upholstered French and English chairs with wooden frames. Larger nail heads can be applied on the edges of a sisal floor covering leading up a stairway.

tassels Tassels by nature add a charming flourish. I like to attach them to keys in the locks of commodes, armoires, or doors. If you are displaying a favorite book on a table, entice passersby to take a quick peek by inserting a tasseled bookmark. Combined with silk rope or cording, tassels serve as lovely tiebacks for draperies, portieres, and shower curtains.

MASTER KEY
E.DORMITORY'S
"Life is made up of little things."
PROVERB

For a different spin on a wintry social gathering, a wine tasting can be an intimate and informal occasion. With the focus on the wine, the food can be simple-some good cheeses and fresh fruit are all you need. Labels from favorite vintages are saved in a scrapbook.

A big bowl filled with corks is a testament to the many bottles enjoyed here.

WINE
HARCOURT BRACE
OXFORD
GRANDS ÉCHÉ-
APPELLATION GRANDS ÉCHÉ
BOUTEILLE Nº 05392
ANNÉE 1990
M
MERUS
2000
1970 CHATEAU PALMER
"91 out of 100"
"95+ out of 100
Palmer is one of the
It exhibits a dark,
emerging, fabulously
licorice, overripe plums
cedar, and minerals.
medium to full body,
firm but silky tannin,
this remains a youthful,
While approachable,
3-5 years of cellaring
first 10-15 years of the
tasted, 6/96."

TIME ON YOUR OWN

Winter weather is not always cooperative. Some days it's too cold to venture outdoors, and you might even get snowed in occasionally. While this may hamper sporting or travel plans, part of the upside of staying indoors is the opportunity to catch up on hobbies and enjoy the pleasure of your own company. In these moments, you can use your hands and mind to create beautiful things for your own home or to give as gifts. You can even develop some means of recording your winter-house memories—through artwork or photography, scrapbooks or journals, or even home videos.

I have a lot of interests, and I relish my Aspen visits—I get to work on all the solitary projects I love so much, even if it means packing them up and hauling them halfway across the country.

I am an inveterate scrapbooker. Each leather-bound scrapbook I create memorializes my travels and interests. Just about anything can end up on their pages: photographs, notes, gift tags, poems, postcards, stickers, excerpts from lectures I've attended, bits of gift wrap, and other odds and ends and personal mementos. The places and things they record serve as inspiration for my own homes, clients' homes, and designer show houses.

I also keep a couple of different journals. It is here I write down things I'd like to remember when I'm old and gray. These musings include reports on books I've read and a few key passages jotted down. The words of artists, fashion designers, decorators, gardeners, philosophers, and witty women of style have all found their way into my quote journal.

Needlepoint is another project that is ideal for the winter house. Tucked away indoors in Aspen, I have created some of my own designs, including an acorns-and-oak-leaves motif and a ski-themed backgammon board designed for a client. Needlepoint can be used for all sorts of items, such as pillows, footstools, decorative bellpulls, and curtain tiebacks. Smaller items—Christmas tree ornaments, stockings, eyeglass cases and belts—make the ultimate handmade gift. You may enjoy similar time spent doing embroidery, knitting, or crocheting; you can essentially enjoy yourself wherever you are.

Reading is my number one pastime. I have enjoyed building my library with books on all the subjects that interest me. I often read sitting on the living room sofa with my dogs for company, or curled up with my latest acquisition in bed in the morning with a cup of coffee.

H

HOMEWORK

SCRAPBOOKING AND JOURNAL KEEPING

For me, life is a collage, and that sentiment is translated to the pages of my scrapbooks and journals. Keeping track of your life by recording memories, events, and thoughts is an important pastime that anyone can do. The process of pasting things into a scrapbook or writing in a journal is a creative endeavor, and the perfect way to spend some time on your own in a winter house. Here are some of my favorite scrapbook and journal topics that you might consider for yourself, if they apply.

book reports Remember books you've read by recording a passage or two or maybe a single quote.

decorating ideas Organize decorating clippings for future plans by categories, such as color palettes, furniture styles, inspiring rooms, upholstery details, or lampshade styles.

decorating schemes Include copies of floor plans with dimensions for rooms in progress, photos of furniture purchased, fabric swatches, and a wish list.

entertaining notes Recall what flowers were on the table, which table settings were used, what wine was consumed, what was served, who attended, and who sat next to whom—this is essential entertaining etiquette and helps you avoid duplication.

garden cycles Photograph your garden throughout the season to provide yourself with a growing history and get a sense of what works and what does not.

gift records Keep track of gifts given and received to remember exchanges from year to year, and indicate whether thank-you notes have been written.

travels Take photos wherever you go—I recommend using a digital camera so you can immediately review your photos to decide what to keep or reshoot.

wardrobe Note clothing styles you like and keep photos and swatches of clothes you own for easier planning of what to put away for the season or which accessories coordinate; photograph any vintage clothes to help you remember what you have.

My private spot for some downtime is our mudroom. This room is an all-purpose kind of place; a sunroom or a porch could also be used to similar effect. The mudroom is equipped with a breakfast table, a corner banquette, and storage for a host of necessities, and it's where our dogs, Darby and Oscar, sleep. Usually, it's just me in there with the dogs and the newspaper. Though a relatively small space, it serves a multitude of functions.

Loving flowers as I do, I like to have a place where they can be arranged and where all the related items—pots, soil, scissors, and frogs can be kept. A wall of antiqued white drawers and cabinets holds floral supplies and table linens. On top of the cabinets rests an eclectic collection of vases and containers. If your own space for storing containers isn't as accessible, you might wish to create a workbook (similar to the one described on page 153) for ease in remembering what you have. Flower buckets and pots are kept under the sink; a skirt was added to hide them. Made of a blue-and-white Swedish toile, it softens the wall of cabinets. The toile's pattern echoes the look of the delft tiles used as a backsplash to the sink. The look of the room is crisp and simple, reminiscent of Carl Larsson's paintings of sun-splashed Scandinavian interiors.

Here in Aspen I don't usually have the pleasure of creating my own flower arrangements, since I often arrive at the same time as my guests. So it is to this room that winter flowers and foliage are brought in buckets by the supremely talented David and Denise Clark to begin making their signature arrangements for a guest-filled winter weekend. The Clarks know what I like when it comes to flowers, textures, and fragrances, yet they still always manage to surprise me with the most amazing combinations of plant materials. While outside everything is barren, snowy, and cold, inside flowers can bring color, texture, fragrance, and a softness and beauty to your home.

The cabinets in the mudroom are home to linens as well as a collection of vases and containers for flowers. This style of storage also provides decoration for the space.

"Life's what's important. Walking, houses, family."

KATHARINE HEPBURN

LITTLE LUXURIES

FLOWERS AND GREENS

As the outdoor garden is barren in winter, we have an opportunity to create a winter garden indoors. Having things inside that are fresh, green, and alive to inspire you is a special treat and, to me, an absolute necessity. David and Denise Clark, the floral designers who work with me in Aspen, never cease to amaze me with their selections and combinations of color, texture, and materials. We work together to create arrangements that always complement my containers and my table settings. "The occasion, the season, and the color palette and style of the room is our first consideration," says David. "The second and more specific is the containers, china, and linens."

In a winter house, arrangements mean more than just flowers—consider bushes, trees, fruits, and berries—and they aren't intended solely for vases. Try a variety of containers. Here are some of my favorite combinations, developed with David and Denise:

- *a silver compote overflowing with pomegranates*
- *a shallow basket filled with grape leaves, grapes, and figs*
- *an arrangement of small galvanized buckets in varying sizes filled with an assortment of seasonal fruits: one with lady apples, one with nuts, and one with clementines*
- *a creamware jug filled with boxwood, skimmia, variegated ivy, and small pink ranunculus*
- *a large Chinese porcelain bowl filled with baby pineapples*
- *a clay pot planted with a miniature cypress*
- *a wooden flat filled with primroses nestled in moss*
- *colored glass fingerbowls filled with white flowers—roses, carnations, narcissus, and anemones—arranged separately or together*
- *an indoor window box or tall planter filled with amaryllis and underplanted with moss*
- *silver julep cups or any collection of small containers filled with white muscari and clustered together or lined up on a mantel*
- *a mix of French tulips and pine branches*

Heading Outdoors

When you walk out through the door of a winter house and pause on the steps, your whole body feels alive as you breathe in the crisp air. For as cozy as it is inside, you must get outside and experience winter firsthand. In Aspen, you are surrounded by so much beauty—mountains, streams, trees, and gorgeous snow—you are naturally drawn to spend time outdoors every day. Depending on your interests and abilities, there is no shortage of outdoor sports to choose from. Alternatively, you might take a break from all the action and take a simple walk into town. When your nose gets cold and your hands a little chilly, all the better for returning to the comforts of your home—a fire, a book, some hot chocolate. This is the cycle of life in a winter house.

Skiing in Aspen is a part of life, and so are the lunch breaks during which everyone has a chance to recap the morning runs.

ON THE SLOPES

Bundled up in their warmest gear, your family might prefer the thrill of a speedy snowmobile or toboggan ride, or perhaps you most enjoy perfecting your ice-skating or snowman-building technique. For us, the wintry motivation is downhill skiing. Should we happen to visit Aspen during other parts of the year, my husband enjoys a few rounds of golf and I like to take long walks with our dogs. But as soon as there is some snow accumulation, the number one focus is getting on that mountain.

There's something about getting into your ski clothes, warming your head with a furry hat, and strapping on a pair of skis that puts you in touch with some great alpine tradition. Sitting on the chairlift or in the gondola high above the trails feels somewhat like an out-of-body experience as you take in the silent beauty beneath you. I like the camaraderie of skiing with others. My husband and I are lucky to have found a husband-and-wife ski-instructor duo, John and Goog Fahey, and we split up into our respective gender pairs and have a great time together. In a town like Aspen, a ski instructor becomes a very big part of your life! Sometimes my instructor and I ski along in a pack with a few girlfriends. Stopping to have lunch at the club on top of the mountain allows for some good chat time. Sometimes it's a short lunch, other times *much* longer depending upon the topic at hand. It's all about just being together.

ASPEN MTN
Völkl
P50

Après ski, everyone is usually tired, but the mood is totally upbeat with the exhilaration of the day's events. As in any ski town, Aspen's restaurants, bars, and cafés are teeming with people in high-gear après-ski mode. We generally have everyone back to the house for a cup of something warm to drink or a glass of wine. The group will disperse and go off to do their own things: a game of billiards, a visit to the Aspen Institute Film Festival, or a quick collapse on the bed before heading out for the evening. When everyone is tired, it's best not to schedule events too rigidly, so we keep things pretty relaxed. I always look forward to getting out of my ski clothes and having a massage and a dip in the Jacuzzi or a hot bath to relieve my tired muscles and aching body.

AROUND TOWN

When I'm not skiing but still want a breath of fresh air, I head to town. It's also a relief to shed those ski clothes and wear something not athletically inspired! While it's a fantastic place year-round, I think Aspen is particularly wonderful during the winter. There are some great places to shop and good restaurants, and there's always a movie festival or a charity event going on when you need a little culture beyond nature. Aspen has an active social and cultural life and there is never a shortage of events and activities. You learn to pace yourself!

Aspen village is just the right size for taking a stroll. During the day, there is the hustle and bustle of people coming back from the mountain, running errands, or shopping. In the evening, lights and candles make the restaurants and shopwindows glow. I often visit the Explore bookstore and its accompanying café if I cut out early from the mountain, and when I have guests in tow we might pop in to the Hotel Jerome or Little Nell at the base of the mountain for a drink. Enjoyable as these jaunts are, they are just diversions. For once the sun starts to go down, it's time to head back to the warmth and privacy of home.

Après ski, that perfect wind-down time. It is the opportunity to relax, take in the view and enjoy one another's company.

"Be intent upon the perfection of the present day."

William Law

HOTEL
J-BAR
JEROME
HOTEL JEROME
100 N. ASPEN ST.
200 E. BLEEKER ST.
500E HOPKINS AVE

BIKE ROUTE
MUSIC SCHOOL <
ABC/SNOWMASS <

Resources

Knowing where to get things is part of my job. When it comes to shopping, I'm not a snob; I believe you have to shop everywhere to find the best. Here are some of my favorite dealers, stores, and catalogs for outfitting a winter house.

ANTIQUES

Alpen Antiks
319 Y AABC
Aspen, CO 81611
970-544-5384

Jacqueline Adams
2300 Peachtree Road NW
Atlanta, GA 30309
404-355-8123

Kenny Ball Antiques
2125 Ivy Road, #7 Ivy Square
Charlottesville, VA 22903
434-293-1361
www.kennyballantiques.com

Lars Bolander N.Y., Inc.
72 Gansevoort Street
New York, NY 10041
212-924-1000
www.larsbolander.com

The Collection
941 North La Cienega Boulevard
Los Angeles, CA 90669
310-659-1882
www.thecollectionantiques.com

D & B Antiques
240 East 60th Street
New York, NY 10022
212-588-8820

Evans & Leonard Antiques
114 Main Street
New Canaan, CT 06840
203-966-5657

The Gables
711 Miami Circle NE
Atlanta, GA 30324
404-231-0734
www.thegablesantiques.com

Gore–Dean
1525 Wisconsin Avenue NW
Washington, DC 20007
202-625-1776

Hastening Antiques Ltd.
7 East Washington Street
Middleburg, VA 20117
540-687-5664

Hollyhock Hilldale
817 Hilldale
West Hollywood, CA 90069

Eron Johnson
451 North Broadway
Denver, CO 80203
303-777-8700
www.eronjohnsonantiques.com

Lief
646 North Almont Drive
West Hollywood, CA 90069
310-492-0038

Little Bear Antiques
2802 Grand Avenue
Glenwood Springs, CO 81601
970-945-4505

McHugh Antiques
607 East Cooper Avenue
Aspen, CO 81611
970-925-4212

The Mews
1708 Market Center Boulevard
Dallas, TX 75207
214-748-9070
www.themews.net

Amy Perlin Antiques
306 East 61st Street
New York, NY 10021
212-593-5756
www.amyperlinantiques.com

Todd Alexander Romano
1015 Lexington Avenue
New York, NY 10021
212-879-7722

Sentimento
306 East 61st Street
New York, NY 10021
212-750-3111

Lee Stanton Antiques
769 North La Cienega Boulevard
Los Angeles, CA 90069
310-855-9800
www.leestanton.com

Toby West Antiques
892 North Fourth Street
Highlands, NC 28741
828-526-1958

Yew Tree Antiques
414 East 71st Street
New York, NY 10021
212-249-6612

BOUTIQUES

Adirondack Country Store
252 North Main Street
PO Box 210
Northville, NY 12134
800-566-6235
www.adirondackcountrystore.com

Adirondack Decorative Arts and Crafts
251 Main Street
Lake Placid, NY 12946
518-523-4545

Adirondack Store and Gallery
90 Main Street
New Canaan, CT 06840
203-972-0221

109 Saranac Avenue
Lake Placid, NY 12946
518-523-2646

Pierre Deux
625 Madison Avenue
New York, NY 10022
212-521-8012
www.pierredeux.com

Gorsuch Ltd.
611 East Durant Avenue
Aspen, CO 81611
970-920-9388

263 East Gore Creek Drive
Vail, CO 81657
970-476-2294

Ralph Lauren
510 East Cooper Street
Aspen, CO 81611
970-925-5147

867 Madison Avenue
New York, NY 10021
212-606-2100
www.rlhome.polo.com

DECORATIVE PILLOWS

Arabelle Taggart
351 East 58th Street, #1R
New York, NY 10022
212-980-6663
www.arabelletaggart.com
By appointment only

EMBROIDERED PILLOWS

Chelsea Textiles
979 Third Avenue, Suite 914
New York, NY 10022
www.chelseatextiles.com

FABRICS AND TRIMS

Brunschwig & Fils
979 Third Avenue, 12th Floor
New York, NY 10022
212-752-2890
www.brunschwig.com

Calico Corners
Stores nationwide
800-213-6366
www.calicocorners.com

Clarence House
979 Third Avenue
New York, NY 10022
212-221-4704
800-221-4704
www.clarencehouse.com

Chelsea Editions
232 East 59th Street
New York, NY 10022
212-758-0005
www.chelseatextiles.com

Cowtan & Tout
111 Eighth Avenue
New York, NY 10011
212-647-6900

Pierre Frey
979 Third Avenue
New York, NY 10022
212-935-3713
www.pierrefrey.com

Hinson & Company
979 Third Avenue, #732
New York, NY 10022
212-688-5538

Nordic Style London
109 Lots Road
London SW10 ORN
01-44-207-351-1755
www.nordicstyle.com

Ian Sanderson
2123 Chelsea Harbour Design Center
Chelsea Harbour
London SW10 OXE
Second Floor, Center Dome
01-44-20-7352-6919

Scalamandré
222 East 59th Street
New York, NY 10022
212-980-3888
www.scalamandre.com

Whittaker & Woods
Represented by Zoffany
979 Third Avenue, #1403
New York, NY 10022
212-593-9787

FRAGRANCE

Agraria
800-824-3632
www.agrariahome.com

L'Artisan Parfumeur
2, rue de l'Amiral de Coligny
75001 Paris
01-33-0-44-88-27-50
www.laboutiquedelartisanparfumeaur.comw
ww.artisanparfumeur.com/fr/index.html

B.Viz Design
Rebecca Vizard
Route 1, Locustland
St. Joseph, LA 71366
318-766-4950
www.bviz.com
Antique fabric sachets

Caron Boutique
675 Madison Avenue
New York, NY 10021
212-319-4888

Caswell-Massey
518 Lexington Avenue
New York, NY 10017
212-755-2254
www.caswellmassey.com

Cote Bastide
Mecox Gardens
962 Lexington Avenue
New York, NY 10021
212-249-5301
www.cotebastide.com

Crabtree & Evelyn
Stores nationwide and internationally
www.crabtreeevelyn.com

Diptyque
www.diptyqueusa.com
171 Maiden Lane
San Francisco, CA 94108
415-402-0600

123 Newbery Street
Boston, MA 02116
617-351-2430

Floris
703 Madison Avenue
New York, NY 10021
800-5-FLORIS
www.florislondon.com

Guerlain
Bergdorf Goodman
754 Fifth Avenue
New York, NY 10019
212-872-2734
www.bergdorfgoodman.com

Jo Malone
150 Sloan Street
London SWIX 9BX
44-20-7730-2125

949 Broadway
New York, NY 10010
212-673-2220

946 Madison Avenue
New York, NY 10021
212-472-0074
www.jomalone.com

Penhaligons
870 Madison Avenue
New York, NY 10021
212-249-1771
www.penhaligons.co.uk

Saks Fifth Avenue
611 Fifth Avenue
New York, NY 10022
212-940-2660
www.saksfifthavenue.com

FURNITURE MAKERS

Crystal Farm
18 Antelope Drive
Redstone, CO 81623
970-963-2350
www.crystalfarm.com

Paul Ferrante
8464 Melrose Place
Los Angeles, CA 90069
323-653-4142
www.paulferrante.com

Formations
8720 Melrose Place
West Hollywood, CA 90069
310-659-3062

Dennis & Leen
8720 Melrose Place
Los Angeles, CA 90069
310-652-0855

Ralph Lauren
510 East Cooper Street
Aspen, CO 81611
970-925-5147

867 Madison Avenue
New York, NY 10021
212-606-2100
www.rlhome.polo.com

Old Hickory Furniture Co., Inc.
403 South Noble Street
Shelbyville, IN 46176
800-232-2275
www.oldhickory.com

John Roselli
979 Third Avenue, 18th Floor
New York, NY 10022
212-593-2060
www.johnrosselli.com

K. Spiegelman Interiors
623 North Almont Drive
West Hollywood, CA 90069
310-273-2255
www.kspiegelman.com

Rose Tarlow
8454 Melrose Place
Los Angeles, CA 90069
323-651-2002
www.rosetarlow.com

Niermann Weeks
The Fine Arts Building
232 East 59th Street, ground floor
New York, NY 10022
212-319-7979
www.niermannweeks.com

LINENS

E. Braun & Company
717 Madison Avenue
New York, NY 10021
212-838-0650

Leontine Linens
5500 Prytania Street, #125
New Orleans, LA 70115
800-876-4799
www.leontinelinens.com
By appointment

Nancy Stanley Waud
8918 Burton Way, #4
Beverly Hills, CA 90211
310-273-3690
By appointment only

MAIL ORDER

B. D. Jefferies
800-954-3004
www.bdjeffries.com

Eddie Bauer Home
800-625-7935
www.eddiebauer.com

Garnet Hill
800-622-6216
www.garnethill.com

Gorsuch, Ltd.
800-525-9808
www.gorsuchltd.com

L.L. Bean Home
800-441-5713
www.llbean.com

The Skiing Company Store
800-815-9236
www.mchalet.net

Source Perrier Catalog Merchants
888-543-2804
www.sourceperrier.com

Sundance
800-422-2770
www.sundancecatalog.com

Whispering Pines
800-836-4662
www.whisperingpinescatalog.com

NEEDLEPOINT PILLOWS

Vaughan Designs
979 Third Avenue, Suite 914
New York, NY 10022
212-319-7070

SCRAPBOOKING SUPPLIES

Archiver's
Stores nationwide
www.archiversonline.com

Creative Memories
800-341-5275
www.creativememories.com

Memory Makers Magazine
Stores nationwide
800-366-6465
www.memorymakersmagazine.com

Mrs. Grossman's
800-429-4549
www.mrsgrossmans.com

STATIONERY AND PLACE CARDS

Smythson of Bond Street
4 West 57th Street
New York, NY 10019
212-265-4573
www.smythson.com
Place cards and invitations

Mrs. John L. Strong Co.
Barneys
699 Madison Avenue
New York, NY 10021
212-838-3775
Place cards and invitations

Tiffany & Company
Stores nationwide and internationally
www.tiffany.com
Silver, glass, and china

Vogel Bindery
PO Box 17
Wainscott, NY 11975
631-329-3106
Leather seating charts

TABLE SETTINGS

Benneton Graveur
75 boulevard Malesherbes
75008 Paris
33-43-87-57-39
www.bennetongraveur.com

WRAPPINGS AND RIBBONS

Hyman Hendler & Sons
67 West 38th Street
New York, NY 10018
212-840-8393
www.hymanhendler.com

Kate's Paperie
Stores located throughout
New York, NY
888-941-9169
www.katespaperie.com

M & J Trimming Company
1008 Avenue of the Americas
New York, NY 10018
212-391-6200

Tinsel Trading Company
47 West 38th Street
New York, NY 10018
212-730-1030
www.tinseltrading.com

Scheme Suggestions

A SCHEME FOR A GREAT ROOM pages 38–39

1. *Ralph Lauren: Maeve Floral Stripe/Tea*
2. *Brunschwig & Fils: Menuiserie Wood Mold Fringe*
3. *Lee Jofa: Carousel Tassel Fringe*
4. *Brunschwig & Fils: Paragon Texture/Beige and Coral*
5. *Ralph Lauren: Victoria Falls Paisley/Eucalyptus*
6. *Nobilis: Derby Wool*
7. *Brunschwig & Fils: Leather 2630.00/3*
8. *Brunschwig & Fils: Millbrook Wool Plaid/Redwood*
9. *Brunschwig & Fils: Adirondack Ash Wallpaper*
10. *Brunschwig & Fils: Wales Woven Texture/Topo*
11. *Ralph Lauren: Macedonia Velvet/Camel*

A SCHEME FOR A DINING ROOM OR A MASTER BEDROOM pages 76–77

1. *Ralph Lauren: Plaid Wool Lincolnshire/Olive*
2. *Lee Jofa: Apollo Linen Velvet/Boxwood*
3. *Ralph Lauren: Wadsworth Paisley/Tan*
4. *Ralph Lauren: Cotton Graham Floral/Camel*
5. *Lee Jofa: Leather/LJ—Bison/Caramel*
6. *Scalamandré: Lattice Tape*
7. *Nobilis: Milord/#2*
8. *Brunschwig & Fils: Horsehair Simone Texture/Multi on Cream*
9. *Lee Jofa: Fan Edge Trim*
10. *Brunschwig & Fils: Chartwell Jasper/Toast*
11. *Ralph Lauren: Cotton Basketweave/Verde*
12. *Brunschwig & Fils: Caravan Pom-Pom Fringe*
13. *Nobilis: Broderie/Cystes*

A SCHEME FOR A BEDROOM pages 114–115

1. *Brunschwig & Fils: Sconset Quilted Floral/Red and Cream*
2. *Brunschwig & Fils: Valreas Check/Red and Cream*
3. *Ralph Lauren: Keswick Paisley/Black*
4. *Brunschwig & Fils: Fiona Cotton and Linen Print/Red*
5. *Pierre Frey: Jimmy/Vert*
6. *Lee Jofa: Twig Print/Cherry*
7. *Ralph Lauren: Ventoux Embroidery/Red and White*
8. *Brunschwig & Fils: Dorsett Tape*
9. *Brunschwig & Fils: St. Kitts Cotton Check/Chili*
10. *Pierre Frey: Alpage/Noir*
11. *Brunschwig & Fils: Nail Head Matte Gimp*
12. *Brunschwig & Fils: Palmino Horsehair Texture/Black*
13. *Pierre Frey: Faux Fur/Fourrure Loup/Original*
14. *Brunschwig & Fils: Les Touches Cotton Print/Black*

A SCHEME FOR A GENTLEMAN'S ROOM pages 134–135

1. *Pierre Frey: Les Trophées/Crème*
2. *Brunschwig & Fils: Tabora Bead Fringe*
3. *Ralph Lauren: Hanley Plaid/Celadon*
4. *Ralph Lauren: Dories Texture/Red*
5. *Brunschwig & Fils: Kennebec/Redwood Wallpaper*
6. *Scalamandré: Wool Fanedge*
7. *Brunschwig & Fils: Izmir Paisley Texture/Burgundy with Rust*
8. *Lee Jofa: Leather/LJ-Country/Saddle*
9. *Nobilis: Milord/#2*
10. *Brunschwig & Fils: Heartland Linen Tufted Gimp/Green*
11. *Brunschwig & Fils: La Seyne Check/Sandstone*
12. *Lee Jofa: Cord T2004751-622*
13. *Ralph Lauren: Old North Corduroy/Bark*

A SCHEME FOR A FAMILY ROOM pages 164–165

1. *Brunschwig & Fils: On Point Cotton Print/Blue*
2. *Ralph Lauren: Dories Texture/Indigo*
3. *Brunschwig & Fils: Bordage Wood Mold Fringe*
4. *Brunschwig & Fils: Oatlands Tapestry/Blue Red*
5. *Brunschwig & Fils: Millbrook Wool Plaid/Baltic*
6. *Ralph Lauren: Old North Corduroy/Cape Cod Green*
7. *Ralph Lauren: Campaign Linen/Blond*
8. *Brunschwig & Fils: Penelope Ball Fringe*
9. *Ralph Lauren: Jute Atlantic*
10. *Brunschwig & Fils: Renoud Texture/Dark Blue*
11. *Ralph Lauren: Stone Hill Gingham/Indigo*
12. *Brunschwig & Fils: Abigail Figured Woven/Blues*

Room Scheme Details

GREAT ROOM/LIVING ROOM

Curtains
Fabric: Clarence House "Silver Jubilee" and "Petite Jubilee" in navy blue
Trim: Hinson & Co. "Gainsborough" braid, cord, and 36-inch tieback
Sofa
Ashley Manor Salon Collection "Charlotte" Sofa
Fabric: Clarence House "Petite Jubilee" in cream/blue
Trim: Hinson & Co. "Gainsborough" 6-inch bullion
Antique scroll armchair
Fabric (front): Brunschwig & Fils "Abigail Figured Woven"
Fabric (back): Brunschwig & Fils "Nantucket Quilted Cotton"
French open armchair
Fabric (front & back): Pierre Frey "La Bussière" (reversible)
Dining chairs
Niermann Weeks "Regence" chair
Fabric: Travers "Samarcand Selections"
Cabinet
Fabric: Clarence House "Petite Jubilee" in navy blue
Sofa
Ashley Manor #970 Sofa
Fabric: Silk Surplus Baranzelli Velvet in tarragon
Breton wing chair and tabouret
Fabric (front): Clarence House "Vet Ireland"
Fabric (back): Clarence House "Changmai" in brown
Trim: (Tabouret): Passementerie rope trim
Kitchen Curtains
Fabric: Clarence House "Petite Jubilee" in navy

FIRST FLOOR POWDER ROOM

Wallpaper
Brunschwig & Fils "Chandigarth"

SECOND FLOOR POWDER ROOM

Wallpaper
Clarence House "Green Three Over Stripe"

MASTER BEDROOM

Primary fabric (on the bed and settee)
Pierre Frey "Coramandel Fond" in crème
Window sheers
Fabric: Chelsea Editions
Wallpaper
Cowtan & Tout "Clover Leaf"

MASTER BATH/DRESSING ROOM

Wallpaper
Cowtan & Tout "Clover Leaf"
Antique side chair
Fabric: Brunschwig & Fils "Chinoiserie à l'Américaine Toile" in plum
Trim: Samuel & Sons cord (in green, purple, and lavender)

GRAY GUEST BEDROOM

Curtains, bed skirt, and bed valance
Fabric: Ian Sanderson "Pym Stripe" in Putty
Trim (curtains only): Samuel & Sons "Jacquard" tape
Slipper chair
Ashley Manor Salon Collection "Laura Chair"
Fabric: Clarence House "Tahiti Charcoal"
Wallpaper
Whittaker & Woods "Yellow Book"

PINK GUEST BEDROOM

Bed
Fabric: Cowtan & Tout "Langham Check" in pink

BLACK TOILE GUEST BEDROOM AND BATH

Wallpaper
Brunschwig & Fils "Chinoiserie à l'Américaine Toile"
Window shades and bed skirts, show curtain
Fabric: Brunschwig & Fils "Chinoiserie à l'Américaine Toile"
Antique Chair and Ottoman
Fabric: Clarence House "Lampas Genet" in noir
Trim: Clarence House "Picot Grosgrain Ribbon" in black
Armoire
Fabric: Brunschwig & Fils "Chinoiserie à l'Américaine Toile"

BLUE AND YELLOW BEDROOM

Bed
Fabric: Pierre Frey "Longueville" in blue and yellow
Lining: Clarence House "Fancy Linen" in blue
Trim: Cowtan & Tout "Fan Edging" in sage green
Trim (headboard): Cowtan & Tout "Narrow Picot Braid" in aqua
Curtains
Fabric: Pierre Frey "Longueville" in blue and yellow
Trim: Cowtan & Tout "Fan Edging" in sage green
Lining: Clarence House "Fancy Lining" in blue
Wallpaper
Cowtan & Tout "Saltram Trellis" in blue

GUEST APARTMENT

Curtains
Fabric: Pierre Frey "Petit Parc" in Jaune 2
Trim: Clarence House "Cyrano Moulinée" fringe
Lining: Clarence House "Fancy Work" in sand
Sofa
Anthony Lawrence Belfair "Knole" sofa
Fabric: Cowtan & Tout "Sedona" in sand/gold
Trim: Scalamandré gold cord, Scalamandré tape
Wing chair and ottoman
Chair and ottoman: Charles Faudree
Fabric: Brunschwig & Fils "Camaldoli Check" in Saffron
Antique caned-back chairs
(at desk in room)
Fabric: Brunschwig & Fils "Crozon Check"
Trim: Brunschwig & Fils "Picot Tape Trim"
Banquette
Fabric: Pierre Frey "Petit Parc" in Jaune 2
Trim: Samuel & Sons Tape

GUEST APARTMENT BEDROOM

Headboard
Fabric: Quadrille "Ragsdale Paisley" in multi-burgundy on gold
Trim: Samuel & Sons
Bedding
Duvet fabric: Scalamandré "Salomé" in yellow rust
Walls
Wallpaper: Whittaker & Woods "Ditchley"

BILLIARD ROOM

Walls
Fabric: Scalamandré "Gunga Din Paisley" in olive green
Trim: Houles "Brianon Barbizon"
Bar stools
Dessin Fournir "Jacob Bar Stool"
Fabric: MHG Studio "Red" Leather

MUDROOM

Sink skirt
Fabric: Nordic Style "Castle Toile" in blue/cream
Curtains
Fabric: Nordic Style "Castle Toile" in blue/cream
Lining/Contrast: Pierre Frey "Escousetto"
Banquette
Fabric: Pierre Frey "Mennecey"

Recommended Reading

There are excellent decorating books to inspire your winter-house mind-set, whether you're actually in the mountains somewhere or just wish you were. Here are some of my favorites.

Barnes, Christine. *Great Lodges of the West.* Bend, Oreg.: W. W. West, 1997.

Carley, Rachel. *Cabin Fever: Rustic Style Comes Home.* New York: Simon &Schuster, 1998.

Gilborn, Craig. *Adirondack Furniture and the Rustic Tradition.* New York: Harry N. Abrams, 1987.

Kyhlloe, Ralph. *Cabins and Camps.* Layton, Utah: Gibbs Smith, 2002.

———. *Rustic Style.* New York: Harry N. Abrams, 1998.

McBride, Simon, and Alexandra Black. *Ski Style: Alpine Interiors, Architecture and Living Style.* New York: Thomas Dunne Books/St. Martin's Press, 2000.

Mulfinger, Dale, and Susan E. Davis. *The Cabin: Inspiration for the Classic American Getaway.* Newtown, Conn.: Taunton Press, 2001.

O'Leary, Ann Stillman. *Adirondack Style.* New York: Clarkson Potter, 1998.

Ryan, Mary Wynn. *Cottage Style.* Lincolnwood, Ill.: Publications International, 2002.

Solvi, dos Santos. *Décors de Bois.* Oslo: JW Cappelens Forlag, 1997.

Stiles, David R. *Cabins: A Guide to Building Your Own Nature Retreat.* Toronto: Firefly Books, 2001.

Teipner-Thiede, Cindy, and Arthur Thiede. *The Log Home Book.* Layton, Utah: Gibbs Smith, 1993.

Thiede, Arthur, and Cindy Teipner. *American Log Homes.* Layton, Utah: Gibbs Smith, 1986.

Wedekind, Beate. *Alpine Interiors.* New York: Taschen, 1998.

———. *Mountain Interiors.* New York: Taschen America, 2002.

Whitesides, Mary, and Matthew Reier. *Mountain Style.* Layton, Utah: Gibbs Smith, 2004.

Index

A
Après ski, 180
Armoires, 94
Artwork, 46, 50–51, 52, 65, 68, 73, 81, 86, 93, 111

B
Banquette, 107
Bath accoutrements, 73, 84
Bathrooms, 52–53, 72–75, 101, 125
Bathtubs, 73
Beads, 168
Bed hangings, 63, 81, 101
Bed linens, 69, 86
Bedrooms. *See* Guest rooms; Master bedroom
Beds, 60–63, 81, 86, 90, 98, 111
Bedside tables, 62, 66–67, 81, 111
Bedspreads, 86
Bed trays, 64
Billiard room, 162, 166–67
Blue-and-Yellow Room, 98–101
Board games, 162
Body lotions, 73, 97
Books, 34, 97, 172, 173
Bouclé, 33

C
Cabinets, 41, 94, 145, 175
Candles, 21, 52, 97, 125
Canopied beds, 60–63, 81
Carafes, 62, 66, 97, 145
Carpets, 93
Carving sets, 145
Cashmere, 33, 34
Ceilings, high, 28–31
Chairs
  bedroom, 66, 81, 93, 94, 101
  desk, 93, 94, 101
  dining room, 41
  fabrics for, 84, 93
  living room, 31
  miniature, 81, 101
  slipper, 74, 84
Chandelier, 74
Chenille, 33
China, 142, 145, 146, 153
Christmas gifts and wrappings, 136–41
Christmas tree decorations, 128–33
Clocks, 46, 68
Closets, 26, 94
Coffee service, 146
Coffee tables, 31, 34
Color schemes
  black-and-white, 90–93
  blue-and-white, 31
  claret, brown, and gold, 111
  pink, 86
Cookies, decorated, 120
Corona, antique, 98
Curtains, 31, 42, 69, 73, 81, 83, 86, 98

D
Desks, 66, 78, 93, 94, 101, 102, 104–5, 107
Dining areas, 40–41, 102, 107
  fabrics, 76–77
  table linens, 145, 150, 153
  tables, 41, 69, 107
  table settings, 142–57
Doors, French, 28
Dressers, 94
Duvets, 93

E
Embroidery, 33
Engravings, 81, 86, 93
Etchings, 46
Evergreens, 18–21, 25, 37, 120, 126–27, 177
Exterior of home, 18–23

F
Fabrics
  bathroom, 73
  bedroom, 62, 76–77, 81, 83, 86, 90, 98, 114–15
  buttery yellow, 98
  chair, 84, 93
  dining area, 76–77
  family room, 38–39, 164–65
  feminine, 86
  floral, 62, 73
  foyer, 38–39
  gentleman's room, 134–35
  great room, 38–39
  living room, 31, 38–39
  paisley, 28, 31
  patterned, 38–39
  ticking stripe, 81, 83
  toile, 84, 90
  upholstery, 84, 93
  winter, types of, 32–33
Family room fabrics, 38–39, 164–65
Faux bois, 146
Felt, 33
Finishing touches and trims, 168
Fireplaces, 37, 66, 101
Flannel, 33
Flatware, 145, 153
Flooring, 26, 46, 69, 93, 101
Flower containers, 37, 84, 175, 177
Flower petals, 125
Flowers, 25, 37, 52, 73, 74, 84, 97, 120, 126, 154, 175, 177
Footstools, 31
Foyer fabrics and patterns, 38–39
Foyers, 24–27, 125
Fragrance, 73, 125, 128
French doors, 28
Fruits, decorative, 120, 177

G
Garlands, 18–21, 120
Gentleman's room fabrics, 134–35
Gifts and wrappings, 136–41
Glassware, 69, 145
Gray Room, 80–85
Great room fabrics and patterns, 38–39
Greenery, 18–21, 25, 37, 120, 126–27, 177
Guest apartment, 102–13
Guest rooms
  Blue-and-Yellow Room, 98–101
  fabrics for, 114–15
  Gray Room, 80–85
  luxuries for, 96–97
  Pink Room, 86–89
  Toile Room, 90–95

H
Hair dryers, 97
Hallways, 46–51, 125
Hangers, 97
Herbs, 42, 45
Holiday decorating, 118–27

I

Inkstands, 60, 68
Inside activities, 162, 166–67, 172–75
Iron gates, 18

J

Jacuzzi, 74
Journals, 137, 172, 173

K

Kitchen, 42–43
Knits, 33

L

Lamps, 86
Lamp shades, 108–9
Lanterns, 21
Lavender scents, 128
Layered looks, 69
Lighting, 74, 86, 108
Linens, bed, 69, 86
Linens, table, 145, 150, 153
Lip balms, 97
Little luxuries
  bed trays, 64
  flowers and greens, 177
  fragrance, 125
  guest hospitality and amenities, 97
  place cards, 156
  tea trays, 44
Living room fabrics and patterns, 38–39
Living rooms, 28–31, 34–37, 102
Luggage racks, 94, 97

M

Magazines, 52, 97
Magnifying glass, 107
Maps, framed, 46
Master bath, 72–75
Master bedroom, 60–68
Master bedroom fabrics, 76–77, 114–15
Matelasse, 33
Mirrors, 52, 101
Mudrooms, 175

N

Needlepoint, 172
Nightstands, 62, 66–67, 81, 111

O

Ornaments, Christmas tree, 128–33
Ottomans, 31, 34, 94
Outdoor activities, 178–81

P

Paintings, 46, 65, 68
Passementerie, 168
Photographs, 111
Pillows, 34, 62, 69, 78, 86
Pink Room, 86–89
Place-card holders, 145, 153, 156
Place cards, 154, 156
Place mats, 69
Portieres, 25, 28
Posters, 46, 50–51
Powder rooms, 52–53, 125
Present journal, 137
Public areas, 46–53

Q

Quilts, 81, 86

R

Ribbon, 168
Rugs, 69, 74

S

Sachets, 97, 125
Scents. *See* Fragrance
Scrapbooks, 153, 172, 173
Seating areas, 31
Secret Santa gift exchanges, 137
Serving pieces, 145, 146, 153
Settees, 66, 86
Shades, lamp, 108–9
Shades, window, 69
Shelves, 111
Sideboards, 41
Skiing, 178
Ski posters, 46, 50–51
Slippers, 74
Soaps, 52, 73, 97, 125
Sofas, 31, 34, 102, 107
Stairwells, 46–51
Storage
  bedroom, 94
  foyer, 26
  mudroom, 175
  table setting, 144–45, 153
Suede, 33

T

Tablecloths, 150
Tables, bedside, 62, 66–67, 81, 111
Tables, coffee, 31, 34
Tables, dining room, 41, 69, 107
Tables, hall, 25
Tableware, 142–57
Tall rooms, decorating, 28–31
Tape and nail head, 168
Tassels, 62, 168
Tea trays, 44
Television, 37
Throws, 34
Ticking stripe, 33
Tiebacks, 62, 83, 86, 168
Tiles, 101
Toile Room, 90–95
Towels, 52, 97
Trays, bed, 64
Trays, tea, 44
Tureens, 145

U

Upholstery, 84, 93

V

Vases, 37, 175, 177
Velvet, 33
Vogue magazines, 52

W

Wallpaper, 38–39, 52, 81, 93
Wallpaper gift wrap, 137–38
Wardrobes, 94
Wastepaper baskets, 54–55
Water carafes, 62, 66, 97, 145
Welcoming gestures. *See also* Little luxuries
  exterior of home, 18–23
  foyer, 24–27
  living room, 28–31, 34–37
Window boxes, 21
Window treatments, 31, 42, 69, 73, 81, 83, 86, 98
Wine cellar, 167
Wood, old, 107
Wool, 33, 34
Wrappings, gift, 136–41
Wreaths, 120

"Winter's done, and April's in the skies;
Earth, look up with laughter in your eyes."
JOHN MASEFIELD